The Missing Piece in Gratitude

Real Stories from Real People

#1 International Best Selling Book Series

The Missing Piece in Gratitude:
Copyright © 2015 by The Missing Piece Publishing
www.themissingpiecepublishing.com

All right reserved. Printed in the United States of American & the UK. No part of this book may be used or reproduced in any manner whatsoever without written permission except in the case of brief quotations em- bodied in critical articles or reviews.

Although the authors and publisher have made every effort to ensure that the information in this book was correct at press time, the author and publisher do not assume and hereby disclaim any liability to any party due to these words coming from the authors own "Personal Opinion" of their experiences.

Every word in this book is based on the authors' own personal experiences of their own personal development journeys, and the outcomes of clients that they may have witnessed Although we have made every reasonable attempt to achieve complete accuracy in the content of this book, we assume no responsibility for errors or omissions if the information in this book happens to be carried out by yourself.

You should only use this information as you see fit at your own risk. Your life and circumstances may not be suited to these examples and what we share amongst these pages.

 The authors and publisher are neither a doctor or in a position of registered authority to give you expert advice. All we can share is what we have tested on ourselves and obtained through witnessing the changes in our lives or our clients' lives along the way.

How you choose to include this information in this book within your own life is completely your own responsibility and own risk.

The Missing Piece Publishing House
36 Seathorne Walk
Bridlington
East Yorkshire, YO16 7QP
England

For information visit www.themissingpiecepublishing.com
Book and Cover Design by Jennifer Insignares www.yourdesignsbyjen.com
Book Formatting by Bojan Kratofil
Proof Reader : Amanda Horan www.gobookyourself.info
ISBN: 978-1-5136-0676-7

Contents

Introduction 1

Chapter 1: True Abundance
By April Adams 6

Chapter 2: Abundance
By Sarah Brink 16

Chapter 3: "From "Growlingtude" to Gratitude"
By Violeta Rajacic 28

Chapter 4: Manifesting Your Ideal Life
By Rosemarie St. Louis 37

Chapter 5: Coming from the soul...
By Wienke Ursula Schulenburg 48

Chapter 6: Gratitude Feels Great!
By Sylvia Friedman 58

Chapter 7: My Definition of Abundance
By Lil Lezarre 68

Chapter 8: The Princess and The Bentley
By Emma Coker 73

Chapter 9: Gratitude for abundance – The Time Traveller's Life
By Jeff Hutchens 82

Chapter 10: The Glocalization of Gratitude & Greater Goodness
By Laurie Vallas 88

Chapter 11: Manifest Abundance Using Gratitude
By Stephanie J. Alvarez 103

Compiled by Kate Gardner

Introduction

"I am always grateful for all that I have in my life. I have a magnificent home. I have a tremendous wife... I love spending time with my family, and I absolutely love what I do in my business every day. I HAVE the best and much to my surprise it keeps getting better".

"BUT the point is I was not grateful when I had no home, no wife, no family and no business. You see it doesn't matter where you are in life. There's a reason right now to express gratitude".

"So do it now. Get into the habit of it. Write your gratitude list every night, or say it out loud in the shower every morning. You'll notice in just a matter of days how long that list begins to grow- and what change in attitude it creates for you... and that's where the attraction finds its way to you"

~Jack Canfield

Gratitude is one of the most important feelings which work in line with the law of attraction. If you learn how to use more gratitude for the things that you already have in your life, then you will notice more good things come your way. Gratitude operates through a universal law that governs your whole life and without it you wouldn't be able to attract abundance.

It's well known that gratitude is the highest expression of love that we can give in this world. History shows us evidently that if we go back through time and notice the sayings of all the great people who lived. For example; Albert Einstein, Wallace Wattles, Beethoven and Napoleon Hill and many, many more have said that gratitude brings you much more. Albert Einstein, who was the greatest scientist who ever lived spoke of giving thanks 100 times each day in order to receive everything that the heart desires.

> *"100 times every day. I remind myself that my inner and outer life depend on the labours of other men, living and dead, and I must extend myself in order to give in the same measure as I have received and I am still receiving"*
>
> ~Albert Einstein

If you learn to use gratitude and be grateful for the circumstances that you have now and learn to use gratitude more in your life on a daily basis. You will be truly amazed by how much you receive back. Your gratitude levels will be at a whole new level, and so will abundance in your life too!

It's exactly how I started out on my journey and I still use it today to remind me of all the things I am thankful for in my life every day. From the moment I wake up to the moment I go to bed I am always in full appreciation of something. I remember the day when it hit me that I actually **"got it!"**

I was mopping my kitchen floor while listening to my mentor Jack Canfield's voice module recording for the coaching program called *The Success Principles*.

This was only the 28th time that I was listening to the same recording, because I was following his instruction of **"Keep listen till you get it"**. So I did! And boy it hit me between the eyes and I stopped what I was doing and dropped the mop handle to the floor. **"Oh my god! I get it!"** From that day forward I placed so much more gratitude into my life and it really worked for me and improved my life and still does today.

The reason using more gratitude works in your life is because when you express gratitude for what you already have you are then putting yourself in the frame of mind that is of joy and expectancy. You are now focusing on what you have, rather than what it is you don't have. This is then sending out the message to the universe that what you have already is a lot and in return the same energy is then returned back to you.

Even on your darkest days you can find something to be grateful for no matter how tiny. You can wake up and go outside to look up to the sky and breathe in deeply and feel a sense of joy to be alive for another day. Keeping your focus upon what it is you feel grateful for at least 15 minutes per day rises your vibration to be in line to attract amazing things too you.

When you are sending out the thoughts and feelings of being un-grateful the law of attraction will just keep returning what you already have. So use this to your advantage and send out the right energy to receive the right things you desire in your life. Everything is energy and everything vibrates, include human beings.

The Missing Piece in Gratitude & Abundance

By learning more about gratitude and vibration we can then learn to focus on things that are truly important and learn to appreciate the value you of them within our reality and keep focusing on that abundant feeling. I am so happy that we decided to bring forward this subject in *The Missing Piece* book series because I feel it is so important for you to read real people's stories and learn first-hand of other people's experiences in their lives, so they can tell you how gratitude has affected their lives and how it has helped them feel abundant and become better people along the journey.

I look forward to birthing this book to the world, so that she we can share more amazing real stories with you. I hope their words give you hope knowing that we are not alone on our journeys and there is always hope for you within the pages of these books.

Welcome to The Missing Piece in Gratitude.
With Much Love & Appreciation
Kate Gardner
CEO of The Missing Piece Publishing.
www.themissingpiecepublishing.com

Compiled by Kate Gardner

April Adams

April Adams is an Emotional Fulfillment Specialist, Author, Divine Channeler, Intuitive Life Coach, Meditation Trainer, and Reiki Master. She is the creator of The Essence Healing System and the author of the book "Essence: Ending Emptiness, Finding Fulfillment."

April has helped countless women, and a few open minded men, to step out of their personal struggles bringing passion, empowerment and fulfillment to their lives. She specializes in combining the power of the mind with the power of the spirit in order to create the best possible life. Working with her fellow Lightworkers to boost their abilities and avoid depletion is her deepest calling. April Adams is the owner of The Retreat on Elm in downtown Manchester NH.

The HealerOfHealers.com

AprilAdamsAuthor.com

FillingYourCup.com

Facebook.com/adamsapril

Chapter 1

True Abundance

By April Adams

For many, there is a gap between desires and your outcome. You have been doing "all the right things." Setting intentions. Reading books. Practicing visualization. Yet you still don't have what you want.

So let's look at some of what you may desire.

- More money
- More romance, sex and intimacy
- A better car and house
- Success
- A job that you find rewarding AND pays well
- A ring
- A commitment
- A child

Now if you had the thing you wanted, how would you feel? This is actually what you seek. The feeling, NOT the thing. You chase the thing to get the feeling, but any feeling you get is temporary, so you just desire more things.

Compiled by Kate Gardner

True abundance comes from having those feelings anyway, regardless of external circumstances.

It is time to find out how to truly receive. From a deeper place than you've ever known before. You are a limitless being of light, energy and divinity. Any sense of lack you possess comes from a deeper connection with the physical world than with your true state.

Here is a meditation you can do, in order to connect with a deeper sense of yourself, the ONEness that you are a part of, as well as your ability to receive. There is an MP3 guided meditation audio at this link, so that you can just surrender to the process even more.

https://goo.gl/qMkph5

- Close your eyes.
- Take a few slow, deep breaths.
- Allow any tension within you to flow downward and out through the soles of your feet.
- Scan your body and energy field for anything you have been carrying around that doesn't serve you, or doesn't belong to you. Let it drop away and dissolve.
- Let go of your shields, barriers and the suit of armor that you energetically wear out in the world.
- Open your palms upward.
- Envision an opening in the center of your left palm.

The Missing Piece in Gratitude & Abundance

- This opening expands inward, creating a channel (or energetic opening) through your hand, wrist and arm, leading into your heart.
- Now imagine this channel continuing out to your right arm and out through a hole in your right palm.
- Next, see the top of your head opening to receive, creating an opening that connects all the way down to your heart.
- Intend to receive this as an activation of your receiving channels.
- Surrender and allow the energy to flow through you effortlessly.
- Experience it opening all of your energy channels, throughout your entire being.
- Tune your awareness into the flow of energy pouring into your left side and out through your right.
- In through the top of your head and out through your heart.
- Allow the universe to flow through you.
- Feel it filling you up. Filling your love cup. Filling anywhere within you that feels empty, to overflowing.
- This creates a dynamic in which you are able to receive all of the blessings and abundance coming to you, having them bless and fill you, then giving you

the ability to share your blessings with others without becoming depleted or feeling a sense of lack.

- Stay with this visualization and feeling for as long as you'd like.
- Repeat daily, especially when you begin to want something outside of you.

This is merely one step of many to creating and understanding true abundance.

The next piece you need to understand is that you are fully able to create the emotions and feelings you desire.

Bring to mind something that you want. It can be an object or an outcome. How would you feel if you had it? What emotion would it bring you?

Try this: https://goo.gl/X8dJBB

- Close your eyes once again and picture a control panel inside of your brain.
- You can mentally create various dials and switches for emotions and brain chemicals.
- Label some with the emotion or emotions you wish to feel.

The Missing Piece in Gratitude & Abundance

- You may also label some with emotions you'd prefer not to feel.
- See yourself turning the ones you don't want down or off.
- Turn the ones you want to feel on and up, to whatever degree feels right to you.
- Enjoy

You are fully capable of creating feelings for yourself. This is true abundance. No physical object or outcome can consistently come through for you in the way that you can for yourself.

I understand that much of this can be hard to swallow after years of living under a completely different set of rules. You've been taught that love, fulfillment, compliments, and happiness need to come from someone or something outside of you.

And I we ask: How has that been working out for you?

Have your needs been consistently met my others? Or do you feel pushy, whiny or demanding while trying to get your needs met?

I am here to bring the greater truth- that the only happiness or fulfillment you will ever feel or have ever felt comes from you. When you receive a gift, it is your judgment of the gift that gives it value, resulting in specific emotions related to that perceived value. When a person behaves a certain way toward you, you mentally assess whether you like or don't like the behavior and create emotion out of that.

You have the choice of perpetually being awash on the sea of reactionism to outside forces, or to choose your reactions, emotions and experiences. This is abundance.

Imagine knowing that your happiness does not depend on one single person or thing outside of you. That you can create for yourself the very feelings you were hoping to get through interacting with something outside of yourself.

I can hear you saying to yourself: "Okay, but that doesn't pay the bills, put food on the table, allow me to travel or fulfill my purpose on the planet."

Here is the interesting part; it is quite likely that it will do those things. Once you stop telling yourself and the Universe that you don't have what you desire, and instead start giving it to yourself, the world becomes a very cooperative place. All of the things you felt were lacking before start to come to you because you resonate with them.

The Missing Piece in Gratitude & Abundance

Resonating with your desires begins with resonating with your higher self.

Whether you call it your spirit, soul, energy, higher self, God-Self, prana, chi, ki or whatever- it all boils down to one thing, it is our very essence. Over several centuries, for various reasons, we have lost touch with our true essences and begun to live primarily from our egos and logical minds. This creates great dis-ease within us. We become frenzied and feel a perpetual sense of lack, fear and loneliness. Learning how to bring our essence back home to us creates peace, bliss, wisdom, and a sense of completion.

Grounding yourself in the way you're about to experience has numerous benefits: it feels good, it connects you with a much deeper wisdom within you, it brings forth healing from within, and a sense of wholeness. When your essence is within you, you feel more complete, experiencing far less addiction and need for external things to fulfill you.

The two primary components of grounding in this modality are bringing your spirit into your body and raising your vibration. Your vibration is the speed at which the molecules of your body and energy field are moving. The goal is to get them to vibrate at the highest possible frequency at any given time, as well as continually developing the ability to raise it to new heights. All it takes is your intention.

There is absolutely no downside to grounding- except that you and your essence are no longer used to it, so it now takes practice and intention to achieve and maintain. However, grounding is the best possible thing you can do for yourself and others- so it's worth the effort. Eventually it becomes easier and more natural and the payoff is huge.

Here is one last meditation to allow you to begin resonating with your desires and your highest self.

https://goo.gl/MnPHht

- Relax in a quiet place.
- Call your spirit essence to you and ask it to enter/merge with your physical body. Allow yourself to experience this in whatever way it comes to you. You may feel something settling in your heart and solar plexus chakra areas. It may also appear to you as a light version of you, stepping into your body.
- Feel the energy filling and surrounding you. Pay close attention to how your hands and feet feel. This will help you recognize when you're "in" later on. Ask and intend for your body and brain to be raised in vibration to resonate perfectly with your essence.
- Observe this process with all of your senses; find out how it feels/looks/sounds to resonate at this higher vibration. Stay with this as long as you'd like.

Practice this technique whenever you think of it, are feeling off, are engaging in energy work, feel unsafe, feel fearful, wish to tap into your intuition, etc. The more you ground, the easier it becomes. Eventually you will be able to ground while walking down the street or having a conversation. This will evolve into spontaneous connectivity over time.

Note:

Your essence is not used to being grounded any more than you are, so it may "pop out" as quickly as it went in- especially if you don't allow your vibration to rise up to meet it and maintain that vibration. It can be quite uncomfortable for our essence to live in our lower vibrational bodies- especially if we are commonly stressed or depressed. Think about how it feels to be around a person who is extremely high or low energy for extended periods. Now imagine trying to live inside their energy field constantly. This is how your essence feels living in a lower vibrational body. Just keep practicing and raising your vibration as much as you can. You'll get it, and before long, your essence will feel right at home where it belongs!

*All links are case sensitive

Sarah Bink

After spending 20 years of her life in a corporate environment helping leaders become the best they could possibly become, she threw in the towel to join her husband on an exciting journey as an expat wife. It came as no surprise to her or her husband that playing the expat wife role was not going to entertain for long and so decided to put her good skills and qualifications to use and became a leadership life coach to people around the world. Her life-long tendency to help people better themselves drove her to write her first book *Rainbows and Rain – Discovering Your Keys To Happiness*, where she teaches many different tools on how to let go of your past live a great life. Today she facilitates workshops on change, coaches clients one on one on living a life of purpose and is currently developing a range of online courses on life changing topics.

On a personal note, she was born in the United Kingdom, was raised in South Africa, has lived in the Middle East and has now settled down in the United States. She loves to run and spend time with her husband and daughter.

Website: www.onlinecoachsarahbrink.com

E-mail: businesscoachsarah@gmail.com

Chapter 2

Abundance

By Sarah Brink

Most of us view the world as a glass half empty. We have been raised to constantly evaluate our expectations, to be cautious not to be overly optimistic.

We choose to rather diminish our expectations by avoiding possible feelings of personal lack and inadequacy, as opposed to striving for abundance. We have lost the essence of who we really are and instead walk through life repeating the same predictable life-cycle patterns as our forefathers – I am not good enough, I do not have enough, or I will never be confident enough to one day triumph over trifling inadequacies.

We constantly compare ourselves to others and beat ourselves up when we discover our shortfalls are mostly imagined. We are disappointed at how easily our self-awareness is swayed to accept the worst. When we do not achieve at the same pace or level as others we label ourselves as a failure. Society reminds us that the only worthy accomplishment is to be Number One. We are raised to believe that second place is the first loser and that constantly striving for the highest rung is what will make us happy and change our view of the world as a glass half empty to a glass half full, only to realise that the glass is never really full. Not everyone has the benefit of a privileged existence; many of us are constantly focussed on scarcity and that brings with it a fear of hopelessness and uselessness. We may focus our attention on the future and give no thought to the here and now. It does not surprise me then, that we have no real concept of abundance. Would we even recognize it if abundance manifested itself before our eyes?

Experiencing lack and discontentment stems from focussing on yourself as a fragmented being, instead of a whole being. External possessions do not result in abundance. Sure they are nice to have, but they are not what truly conveys the essence of abundance. I have been privileged to have lived in very poor countries, where people have no running water and very little money or food, yet I saw them smiling and laughing, helping others in need, and imparting wisdom to their children. Despite their struggles, they were happy with who they are inside. I saw the joy and elation on their faces when they are able to celebrate the gift of a meal. To them, the fact that they could feel satisfied even for only one night is abundance. They lived in the here and now, making the most of the moment, and making every moment count.

I have also witnessed a lady who was a highly motivated professional, type A personality who drove results in her business. Her main focus was on making her organisation a success so that she could be the best executive in her field. She spent countless hours at work, ate very little and spent next to no time with her family. She pumped herself with caffeine and pain pills to counteract the exhaustion and muscle ache that her body was screaming. To her being the best was abundance. She realized that she had gone too far when she was diagnosed with fibromyalgia, a debilitating condition that can be triggered by extreme stress. She was forced to quit her job and rest. In this instance we can see that external satisfaction can result in a lack of abundance. She was living her life as a fragmented being, neglecting all the aspects of self.

I have spent many years trying to understand the concept of abundance. What is abundance and how can we attain it? Is it something that we can realize, or is it an attraction that we aspire to grab hold of like a piece of candy tied to the end of a string? Is my understanding of abundance the same as yours or is it what is perceived through the eyes of the beholder? It was only when I realized that abundance is not a concrete thing, not money or happiness or love, but rather all of these things rolled into one, that my life started to change. We all have our own ideas of what abundance is. The people I mentioned who endured poverty yet were grateful for a meagre meal, knew what abundance was; the executive portrayed being the best in her field as her personal abundance, even though to others, it may represent lack.

As an intuitive coach, I have spent countless hours developing my self-actualization, learning about who I am and really being a student of the universe. Not always an easy road. During this learning process I have come to understand abundance through the essence of I AM. It wasn't until I sat in front of another person and did an exercise on Who Am I, that I realised my whole concept of abundance was very skewed.

The whole exercise started off on a very superficial level, but as the process developed it became quite apparent that this was an exercise that would move from shallow to profound thought. It went something like this.

Who Are YOU?

Well, I am a mother, a daughter, a wife, an Executive Coach, a woman….

Who Are YOU?

Um, I am healthy, I am fit, I am educated, and I am a business owner…

Who Are YOU?

Wow, this is starting to get difficult. I don't know. Um - I am loving, I am kind, I am helpful, I am funny….

Who Are YOU?

Oh boy, I don't know.

Who Are YOU?

The tears started to stream down my face. About two minutes passed and I finally said, I am sad, I am lost, I am hurt.

Who are YOU?

The walls of my mind felt like they were completely stripped away. I sat there sobbing my heart out. I realized that who I thought I was, was only a small part of me. I was so much more than I had ever imagined. So, with tears in my eyes and joy in my heart, I looked at the person in front of me and said – I AM, I just AM.

It was not until a few years later that I realized what I had said on that day. I AM, is everything. It is not one thing or the other, it is all. There are no polarities in I AM, just oneness. Oneness with the universe, oneness with all that is. It just is! It is all, and therefore abundant.

How then can we view the world or ourselves as half empty or even half full and focus on our lives as inadequate, when we have the I AM inside of us? The operative word here is HALF. The all that is, the all that ever will be. When we realize that we have abundance within us, that we ARE abundance, our world view can change. The language of inadequacy or lack can no longer exist. How can we criticize or judge our lives when the I AM essence is our complete make-up?

Abundance is not externally driven, it is internally motivated. It's a way of thinking and a way of living. It is looking at yourself and realizing that you have all the potential and all the skills to live a life filled with all that you need in the world that you create. It is not about comparing yourself with what already exists but about creating something unique. It is happiness, gratefulness, love, joy, and peace, but it is simultaneously pain, sadness, and hurt. It is wealth, it is poverty. It is balance in all aspects of the self. We need to allow our light to shine from within. We have been given everything we will ever need to make a success of our lives, to embrace our purpose. We were born with abundance and carry the light of abundance within us. There is no place for darkness or emptiness when it is filled with abundance. There is no place for lack or limitation. We need to celebrate what is right with the world, instead of judging what is wrong. We need to see ourselves as being good *for* the world and not *in* the world. Abundance is all that is. Abundance is your inner light. Abundance is your I AM.

So how do you create this new frame of mind? How do you go from a place of lack to a place of abundance? How do you identify with your subjective perception when all we have ever known is external? All that we believe we are is driven from an external environment. Focusing instead on the soul source is not an easy thing to change. We need to begin this search by going inward. Unpack your understanding of what you understand to be abundance, how our culture or programming has allowed us to feel inadequate and incomplete. Start by spending time in meditation to understand the limiting beliefs that you have about yourself. Change those beliefs to something that serves your highest good. Listen to how you speak to yourself. Is it a language of lack or a language of abundance? Change what is needed. Be mindful. Mindfulness is being consciously aware of everything instead of being stuck in your mind. You owe it to yourself to be aware of what you are capable of, of who you really are and how you portray that identity in everyday life. Do the exercise repeating the Who Am I question. Strip away the confining barriers. Accept the thoughts and feelings that enter your mind without judgement or fear. If they no longer serve you, ask them to leave and replace them with abundant thoughts. See your world as your playground, and you the director of the movie where you are in control of the outcome. Be present in all you do and practice the art of gratitude. Let go of anything that is judgemental or critical of self. We are very hard on ourselves and beat ourselves up for the smallest things. Often it is a form of procrastination. We would never treat another human being the way we treat ourselves. Live in the now. Spend time in nature and see what she has to offer you. Her world is abundant and she is waiting for you to notice. Go within, meditate, pray or do anything that will connect you to Source. Breathe. You have been given an abundance of breath, the life force energy. Breathe deeply. Give yourself an abundance of love. You deserve to be loved. You are love. You are all that is.

With the new understanding of abundance, comes gratitude. Once we understand the essence of I AM, we can appreciate the external gifts that life gives us every single day. Our world view changes for the better. Life has a tendency to trap us into a rut where we become so focused on day to day living that we forget to actually sit back and acknowledge what we actually have and who we actually are. I once did an exercise that I encourage you to do as well, where I asked a client to think about everything that he perceives as abundant and how that abundance has a positive outcome on his inward existence. It was interesting to watch his reaction when he thought of the question. We are very good at saying what abundance we have externally, but never really give much thought to the internal abundance we carry.

When we still the mind, and sit for five or ten minutes just focussing on our breathing, we are reminded to bring ourselves back into the now. I remember sitting in my living room doing this exercise before the day began, just breathing and focussing on the now, with the intention to focus on what I am grateful for. What I was not intending to experience was the vast amount of things I take for granted every day. I recognized the importance of acknowledging the many tangible things that were representative of abundance that came into my thoughts. Giving thanks must become a spontaneous response. I was reminded that I was sitting in an air conditioned home, on a comfortable chair in clean clothing, with no pain in my body. That in itself begs for gratitude. The deeper I looked the more I discovered and the more I realized how grateful I was to the people that helped me have those gifts, a charmed lifestyle I take for granted. I gave thanks to the men and women who built the home, the companies that produce the electricity and clean water; the man who delivered my new couch and for the men and women who made the couch. I went so far as to thank the people who grow the cotton to provide raw material to textile mills to produce the fabric so that seamstresses can make the clothing that are sold in retail stores; and so my list went on. When you think about it, really think about it – every single item, person or animal in our lives provides abundance. It is up to us to open our eyes and see it. Yet we are programmed to take most things for granted. We blame our habitual acceptance on our busy lives. We no longer see or appreciate what is in front of us. We are so busy striving for something new, different or to accumulate even more of the same. But when is enough, enough?

Human nature is programmed in such a way that we unconsciously strive for better things. What once was the ultimate goal now seems inadequate. What we were once happy with no longer makes us happy. We have become complacent and convince ourselves that finding more will satisfy our search for meaning. This is the perpetual cycle that drives us to become depressed, unhappy and full of lack. Now don't get me wrong. I am not saying that we should all just sit back and accept the status quo and ignore or bury our desire to grow and strive to be better. What I am saying is in order to enjoy the moment that you have worked so hard for, you must also enjoy the abundance of what you have achieved and be grateful for all you are and all you have.

Why? Because logic says so and it's a scenically-proven fact! Much research has been done on the subject of gratitude. One such researcher named Robert Emmons discovered that practicing gratitude on a regular basis actually improves our well-being and satisfaction about life in general. It also has a positive effect on our body; it helps us sleep better; be in a better mood; feel happier about life and feel content. So how do you actually practice gratitude without it becoming repetitive or boring?

Focus on something different every day – when I first started practicing gratitude the same things kept repeating themselves. Today I am grateful for my husband, the food we eat and the money in the bank. Day two – well, I'm still grateful for my husband and the money and the food! Until it became repetitive, and started to sound a tad insincere. Instead of rambling off the same list, pick a topic or area to focus on that is different from yesterday or the day before. Day one – today I am grateful for the way my husband makes me laugh. Day two – I am grateful for the garbage disposal van who removes the trash from our yard. Day three – Today I am grateful for the rain, which has blessed the plants with free water. It is however essential that you are truly grateful for the things you choose to give thanks for. Eventually you will find your acknowledgements are spontaneous.

Look for creative ways to practice gratitude – we are all free spirits and most of us don't like to be tied down to one way of doing things. Think of a few ways you can practice gratitude without becoming bored. For an example – journaling, singing, poetry, art, post-it notes, talking about it at dinner; sending someone a letter. Just telling someone that you appreciate their kindness will not only warm your heart, but will also lighten their day.

Focus on the benefits and not the features of gratitude – what are the real benefits to the things or events you feel grateful for? Benefits are long term and features are short term. For example – I am grateful for the clean water I have in my home because it allows me to keep my body healthy without having to worry about whether I am going to get sick.

Give Back – there is nothing more rewarding and satisfying to help you experience abundance than serving those who have far less than you. Be it money, clothing, food, shelter or teaching someone a useful skill that they can apply to enhance their life. When you work in the community and do something for someone else you feel grateful on many different levels. Giving back teaches you that your glass, no matter how small, is overflowing and that what we take for granted is someone else's wish.

In my book *Rainbows and Rain – Discovering Your Keys to Happiness*, I share a story of how from time to time we need a wakeup call to remind us just how lucky and abundant we really are. It is a story about a facilitation workshop I was conducting on a cold winter's day. We were all in the lounge area, overlooking a beautiful view, in front of a fire place, sipping coffee. The conversations were all about the weather and how miserable it was and how cold we were. During the conversation we noticed a man outside in the distance, walking in the freezing cold. He had torn shoes and no shirt. Freezing cold, the man walked in the street. He had no warm clothing to wear. It became very apparent how quickly everyone became quiet and turned inwards, as if they were embarrassed by their bickering. What they first interpreted as lack, the man in the cold could only have seen as abundant.

Count your blessings every day, especially the ones you take for granted. Give thanks for your sight, hearing and speech; the ability to walk, and comprehend important lessons about recognizing abundance.

Compiled by Kate Gardner

Violeta Rajacic

Violeta Rajacic earned a diploma in Business Management. For the past ten years she has been stay-at-home parent. She volunteered for a local Food Bank, Outreach for a local Street Church and does Crisis Peer-Mentoring. Four years ago when a tragic event shattered her world, leaving her a single mom, she realized it was time to take inventory and examine every broken piece of her heart and soul.

Feeling unloved and abandoned in the worst possible way, she discovered what God's love for her is, which led her onto the path of self-love and finding that "missing piece". This is her story…

Facebook: Violeta Rajacic

E-mail: violeta_rajacic@live.ca

Chapter 3

"From "Growlingtude" to Gratitude"

By Violeta Rajacic

We all want to be exempt from hard times. It's human nature, to seek the path of least resistance and instant gratification. No one asks to have calamity in their life, but what do we do when it strikes? Do we grumble and complain? Do we ask "why me?" Do we play the victim, getting irritated by everything and everyone around us? Do we start lashing out? Do we become depressed and hopeless?

I don't know about you dear reader, but that is exactly how I used to react to life's curve balls. Looking back over the last 25 years, and not in any particular chronological order, here is a quick rundown of my life experiences: my country of origin ceased to exist while I was abroad learning English. For a period of a few years, I wondered if I would ever be able to go back and see my family and friends again. Those fearful feelings of being alone, feeling lost and sorrowful, were all mixed together to form a poisonous cocktail. It was something I would drink daily for a long, long time. I have lost 4 significant people in my life to suicide; I went through a personal bankruptcy; I dealt with a bout of "major depression" after my father passed away (of natural causes); and my relationship with the love of my life was the epitome of dysfunction. For a period of time, I even turned to a bottle looking for relief and answers.

In the second month of pregnancy, I lost my new job and my relationship on the same day. Six months later I ended up homeless and was forced to go on social assistance. Without many options, I ended up living in an RV where the floor was simply boards running from one side of the frame to the other. You could see the ground below them. There were no working appliances of any kind, and there wasn't even a toilet. My bed was a 4" foam pad atop a sheet of plywood, on the makeshift floor. At the same time, the father of my child decided to move in with another woman and refused to help me out. By the grace of God, I managed to get into a new home three weeks before I gave birth. After our son was born, my ex and I went through a custody battle. We ended up managing to co-parent and communicate for a period of a few years. During this time, we maintained a physical and emotional connection even though he was still living with this other woman. We were working through things and I decided to take him back only to lose him again, to a short fling with a different woman and finally, his suicide. At the time I was unaware, but that was just the beginning of a time where I would have many "feeling sorry for myself" pity parties and I would sit in my "soiled diaper" until my behind was starting to "burn", hypothetically speaking of course. The only abundances I felt I possessed were an abundance of things, feelings and experiences that I didn't want. I would get angry and feel depressed with life and the particular circumstance or a person without realising that I actually had complete freedom and power of faith in The Lord and I could choose what to feel about it. I couldn't change the circumstance in some cases, but I could certainly change how I felt about them. Anger is what I didn't want to feel anymore. That feeling, even though it was so familiar, didn't serve me for anything positive. If anything, it blocked any good that could have been coming to me, ever, and it drained the life out of me. So I decided to put on my "big girl panties" and allowed that knowledge to sink in. It took a good decade of reading self-help books, going to counselling, and most importantly accepting my Christian faith. I stopped asking "why me Lord?" Instead I would ask "Lord, what do you want me to do with this? What can I learn here? Where is the silver lining? How do you want me to use this experience? How can I feel grateful for this?"

How do we find that "silver lining" or "blessing in disguise" through our personal tragedies: the loss of a loved one, a job, a divorce, a betrayal, a bankruptcy, an illness, and not to mention the devastating loss of everything through a war or natural disaster? How do we feel abundant when all we see is the" lack-of" in our lives? Sure, we can continue to focus on things we do not have or like but that kind of thinking carries the underlying assumption that we do not have the key to gratitude. A key which, as I already mentioned is the freedom of choice and the power of faith within.

If you ever feel like you are lacking and "you're too broke" to give anything I would encourage you to go through your closets. I'm sure you will find at least a thing or two you can give away to a local homeless shelter. If giving possessions away is not your thing, time is just as valuable of a gift to give; if not more precious. If it's not time or material things, and you are in the position to give someone an opportunity of any kind, it could be a life changer for that person. It is through our giving that we are able to receive. I'm not saying that you should expect anything in return. What I'm talking about is an intrinsic reward, the feeling that can never be lost or stolen. That is the seat of abundance; the internal well, that no matter what, never dries up. It is always there and flowing, one just has to find the way to tap into it. Understandably so, for some people that seems like an impossible task because the hardest things to adjust are things of our internal nature. We don't like to change from the inside. We would rather try to control and change things on the outside hoping that will bring us happiness and success. We often associate abundance with material possessions and only give gratitude when we are blessed with what we've been asking for. That is limiting abundance. It comes in different shapes and forms and often we don't even realize it. Giving gratitude in times when we least feel like it is the time when we need to give it the most. I understand the last thing one wants to do when the dung has been spread all over one's face is to be grateful for it, but that is the key, believe it or not, in learning how to graciously receive.

They say gratitude changes everything and it certainly took a long time for me to understand that concept. As soon as I internalized what it meant to be truly grateful for the life I have been given and the plan that Lord has for me, the doors started opening. Opportunities presented themselves one after another and I could feel the gratitude starting to grow deep inside of my heart. I started to love Life and my role in it. Essentially, I started cleaning out my closets; literally and figuratively speaking. That process took a long time because I had tons of "stuff" I used to surround myself with. Clothes, shoes, accessories and nick-knacks were my thing. There was no room in my closet or in my house for anything new to come in. I had to start letting go. I gave away bags and bags of stuff, dropped my "entitled attitude" and fear of the "lack of", and started thanking the Lord for all that I did have. Even for the things and feelings I only wanted and didn't yet have. Forgiveness was like the "fragrance of a violet I wanted to release on the heel of the one that crushed me." The list of people I felt I needed to forgive was a mile long. That took a while to get through. Patience was definitely something that was slow in coming to me, but it did finally arrive and safely nestle in my heart. Peace was soon to follow and sooner than later, I pretty much got everything I had been asking for. The fact that you are reading this is a miracle in itself. All of my life I dreamed of becoming a published author. Five years ago I even created a social media account where I declared myself an author. At that point I had no idea of how that was going to come to pass but I started thanking the Lord for the opportunity, even though it wasn't there yet. I had some written work but I was not ready to "come out" with it. As it happened, the opportunity met destiny at an event I attended years later, and voila! You are reading it! Three years ago if someone would have told me that I would publish two chapters in two different book collaborations, all within three months, I would probably laugh it off as an "I only wish". Three years ago if someone told me that my son would be attending a private Kelowna Christian School, I would have said the same thing. As far back as the day my son was born, I wanted to be able to provide him with the benefit of attending a private Christian school. At the time I had very limited income and I had no idea of how I was going to make that happen. His father passed away just before our son entered grade one and I had to accept the fact that he would be entering public school system freshly traumatized, to boot. I sucked it up and decided to give it a shot and see how he would be treated considering he had started to display the common behaviours of anxiety. That did not go well for anybody.

After he finished grade three in public school, our son openly disliked school and started showing signs of stress through tummy aches and headaches. That was when I decided to switch schools. By the grace of God, the opportunity met destiny again, and I was shown the way to put him in Kelowna Christian School for grade four and five. That was the biggest blessing in his young life because it changed him completely. His symptoms of anxiety diminished significantly, he improved grades in leaps and bounds, his ability to focus and concentrate came back a good 80%, and most importantly, he feels loved and accepted. The way his new teachers treated him was full of kindness, and gentleness. They set structures in a loving way; giving him the space he needed to process his feelings and supported him in his learning.

After his father's passing, he attended counselling for a short period of time. Since enrolling him in Christian school he has not asked to see his counsellor. Today, he is a well-adjusted and happy boy. This is definitely the biggest thing I am grateful for; my son's happiness, health, and well-being. It takes a village to raise a child and whoever said that was not joking. With that saying in mind, I feel tremendous gratitude for Kelowna Christian School, Metro Church and Metro Community, Pastor Barry of Evangel Church Children's Ministry who has taken the role of a mentor in my son's life and started The Mentoring Program for Fatherless Children since. None the less I extend my gratitude to Dr. Shylon Matthew and Dr. Natalie Matthew of ToothZone Kids for all of their generosity and care, my dear friend Lorelei who has embraced us as part of her family, Kimberly Wallace of Sabey-Rule Law Office for all she has done to make our lives easier, my dear friend and sister in Christ Robyn, and last but not least, the workplace of my late spouse for all of their big-heartedness, love and care. I thank dear Lord for all of them daily.

Today, I take my time analysing each experience as it comes. I use the knowledge gained from my past experiences to strip away the layers of each new" opportunity" to find the silver lining, or core lesson I must learn. Sometimes the experience comes disguised as a "blessing" and it is equally important for me to analyse and not rush into. I am still a work in progress and I thank Lord for that too. He continues to work on my life. With each heart opening experience, my ability to give and receive becomes deeper, so does my gratitude for the happenstances of Life.

"Even a tree has more hope. If it is cut down, it will sprout again and grow new branches. Though its roots have grown old into the earth and its stump decays, at the scent of a water it will bud and sprout again like a new seedling."

~Job 14:7-9

"Do not store up for yourselves treasures on earth, where moths and vermin destroy, and where thieves break in and steal. But store up for yourselves treasures in heaven, where moths and vermin do not destroy, and where thieves do not break in and steal. For where your treasure is your heart will be also."

~Matthew 6:19-21

Rosemarie St. Louis

Rosemarie St. Louis is a Transformation Coach and Yoga Teacher. She loves working with women to manifest abundance, happiness and health and to help them connect to and align with their true joy as she feels that it is from this place that everything works and flows! She is also passionate about gently guiding women to utilise their intuition to tap into their inner guidance to bring about the changes they REALLY want in their lives.

www.intuitivegroundedcoaching.com

https://www.facebook.com/Intuitivegroundedcoaching

https://twitter.com/rosemarieyoga

http://instagram.com/rosemariestlouis

http://www.pinterest.com/strosemarie

Compiled by Kate Gardner

Chapter 4

Manifesting Your Ideal Life

By Rosemarie St. Louis

I recently had an email into my inbox which straight away made me feel, well, how can I describe it? *'less than'*.

I felt alienated somehow because the sender, a 'manifesting expert', wrote that he didn't feel that people could teach about manifesting unless they had successfully manifested …and then he proceeded to list a whole raft of items which he had manifested.

I have no problem with his list of achievements, it was a wonderful list and to be fair I have achieved loads with manifesting - both consciously and unconsciously. I had already achieved some of the things that was on his list too. However, not the £2 million house. Yet. But then I haven't been focussing on manifesting a £2 million house.

See that's the thing with manifesting, we are all manifesters and we manifest all the time. We manifest what we want and what we don't want. Because we get what we think about. So if we are thinking negatively, guess what? We attract negativity to us. If we are constantly thinking, planning, dreaming, visualising, talking about, and working towards getting a £2m house (for example) then, guess what? One day you WILL be sitting in a £2M house - if, and only if, it is the right thing for you and your higher purpose and is good for you as well as for others.

The Missing Piece in Gratitude & Abundance

I know, I know, a little bit cooky - maybe.

See the thing is this. I am sure you have received something that you really really wanted.

For example, for years I wanted to work part time and have a couple of days for myself running my own business. The time never seemed right and I told myself we couldn't afford it. (I say told myself, because that is what we do all the time; tell ourselves stories);

Anyway, I digress, my point is; right now, I am writing this from home in my bright, light kitchen on my MacBook Air with views over the garden. The house is completely quiet, my 12 year old is at school and I have two days off a week to work on my business. I even decided in advance that I didn't want to work Fridays in my next job. And guess what? I even got to choose the days I work! So for two days a week I get to coach women around manifesting an abundant, healthy life as well as teach yoga. And the best thing, unlike my previous roles, when I'm not at my day job, I am not constantly checking my work phone (I don't have one! Yipee!). So it's the kinda job that when I am not there I am free to pursue my passions which is exactly how I wanted it. *Plus* I have always wanted to be a writer and here I am writing this chapter of a book!

So back to that email stating that only a certain kind of person can teach about manifesting. I don't agree. See, we can all teach about manifesting because we ALL manifest ALL the time. Yes, you too. You can teach me the way you do it because only YOU can manifest as YOU.

Just take a moment now. Inhale through your nose and take a deep breath in. Exhale out of your mouth making the sound AHH. Repeat this twice.

Now think about a time when you manifested something that you really wanted. You may have noticed that you thought about whatever it was a LOT beforehand. Identify the processes you went through. Make a note because these are ways that manifesting works for YOU.

YOU are a master manifester because you have done this hundred's maybe thousands of times in your life.

So if we can all manifest what we want, how come we are not all living the life of our dreams right now.

Well there are some provisos and some guidance that it helps for you to follow.

Here's my take.

The Universe

Firstly, let's start with the Universal principles. It helps if you believe that there is a power source greater than you. The Universe is your friend and has your back. We are meant to live our lives on purpose and have all the things that support our dreams and desires for good in the world. We are meant to be happy and to have fun. And the Universe wants to support all of that.

The Universe is Unlimited and when I learned this it kinda blew my mind. So if we match our thinking with *unlimited thinking* then we can create anything we want. Whatever we can imagine can be created. So at the beginning of this chapter I mentioned that I had manifested loads of things sometimes consciously and sometimes unconsciously - the truth is we all do this. When we are not consciously manifesting we are manifesting stuff any way (good and bad) just without putting much thought into it. But we still receive from the Universe because the Universe is always striving to make us happy and give us what we want.

Everything is energy and we are made up of particles of vibrating matter closely packed together. The energy around us is loosely packed. This means that both we and the Universe are one. We are connected. So the Universe provides us with a reflection of our feelings and thoughts.

We create using our feelings and emotions. So if you say you want to have a million dollars but you don't ever feel like a million dollars then the Universe isn't going to send you a large amount of money anytime soon. Because you're not resonating at the frequency of a million dollars. The Universe pays attention to our feelings and gives us what is a vibrational match.

So what do you want?

When I work with women on abundance the first point that comes to me is always what do you really want?

This is where you get to be super clear on what your intentions and desires really are. But even more important is knowing the *essence of your desires.*

I can't stress this enough! It's so important to get clear on the ESSENCE of your desires. Really, really drill down on WHAT is behind your goals.

What this means is getting clear on the needs and higher qualities that you want to fulfill. For example, you might desire a new set of clothes because you have been feeling unconfident at work lately. *So the essence of your desire is that you want to feel more confident.* Once you become clear on the essence of your goals you can start to do something about that.

The Universe may deliver a confidence course - and a new wardrobe won't be required. Does that make sense?

Also, once you become clear on the essence of your desires, it makes it easier to achieve satisfaction and fulfillment and you can more easily recognize when the Universe has delivered your dream outcome to you.

This in turn can save you time, heartbreak AND money!

Being Specific

Once you know the essence of your desires it's time to get *specific* about what you want. It's key. It's no good wanting to be rich. How rich? And what does being rich mean anyway? Get really specific about exactly what you want. If you know it would be great to manifest £5000 to pay off that credit card debt, then start with that. You know just how good you will feel when you are able to pay that amount off. You know that once cleared you can start to put something small aside in your savings and have more financial freedom. And of course once you have achieved that goal you can celebrate and then set a new goal and move towards that.

Plus it's so much easier to connect the dots when you know what you're dealing with. So if your Aunt Mary calls tomorrow (totally out of the blue) and offers you an interest free loan for exactly £5000 you will straight away see the connection and *know* that this is the Universe aiming to give you what you want. You can then smile, say thank you and graciously accept.

[Gratefulness is a major part of manifesting. Learning to use gratefulness *before* we have even received something is very much a principle in the Law of Attraction because we are raising our vibration to a whole new level. But that's another story!]

Intuition

Intuition is totally linked to your manifesting journey.

Your inner guidance is like your **internal compass**; also called intuition or sixth sense. It guides you to the right choices and to whatever is for your highest good.

The ability to work from this extra sense gives you access to **a third dimension** where you can glean information and call upon support that is readily available. When you don't utilise this gift, you are in effect operating from a space of disconnection.

As you work with energy and learn to draw abundance to you, pay extra attention to your inner guidance for this will give you access to greater sources of information, situations and synchronicities that will bring your desires to you. Also pay attention to any dreams that you have and write them down.

Heighten your awareness so that you notice what is going on around you. Otherwise, the Universe may deliver your desire to you but you may not notice.

Guidance is great - but do you act upon it when it shows up? Do you understand the difference between intuition and your head or ego?

When you operate from your intuition, everything feels expansive and joyful, your energy field opens up. If it is your mind or ego then your energy field contracts or closes down.

Also the voice of your intuition is a small, quiet voice and will only give you a couple of steps. For example, your intuition might say; 'Do that'. It won't be like "if you do this you will get this, this and then you will be able to do that" Your heart or intuitive voice will only give you a step. You have to trust and take that step and see where it will lead you. Your ego voice will be the complete opposite of this.

So get clear on what you want & understand the essence of your desires. Start focusing on your feelings and emotions and what brings you joy. Decide to take inspired action utilising your intuition. Focus on what you want and not on what you don't want. It is at this point that you can sometimes self-sabotage.

For example, when money starts flowing in you might feel guilty. This will REPEL abundance. Understand that you deserve your goodness and practice asking for MORE. This is not being greedy, it's just letting the Universe know that you have the capacity. Think of creative ways that you can allow all this goodness in. For example, in a business situation, could you use a VA to spread the work if the work is becoming very busy? Or if you are a yoga teacher with an overbooked class could you have 2 classes one after the other to maximise your time and efforts spread the load? In this way you are welcoming MORE.

If you let the Universe know you can handle more it will send you more. Right?

This is about learning to ALLOW abundance and money to come to you. Know that you are successful and that you deserve that success. You must be in receiving mode for this to take place.

We self-sabotage in other ways too. Procrastinating when we have great opportunities in front of us for example.

I am grateful when I find a penny on the street. Acknowledge every penny that you receive and thank the Universe for it. This goes for your wage packet; and, if you're married, your partner's money too. In fact, any money that comes into you daily. Even if you're not fully happy with your wages. Learn to be grateful for what you have as this will raise your vibration and attract more in due time.

Of course what I have come to realise is that the Universe is sending us abundance all the time and the reason we are not receiving it is because we put blocks and barriers in the way. What is blocking you? Fear? Lack of confidence? Not feeling worthy? Are you giving your power away?

An obvious block would be the way you were brought up around abundance and money. Money is a really emotional subject. And it's worth spending time thinking about your own childhood and the way you were brought up in relation to money. Were your parents always worried and stressing about money? What was your childhood like regarding money? I usually get clients to write a story about how they were brought up around money.

I have come to realise that one of the greatest things that you can do regarding abundance is being true to YOU.

By aligning with what is true to you and the message that you are trying to give out in the world. For example if you have always felt that you have a burning story to tell, it might be time to align with your message and get it out there. Who knows, once your story is out in the world, you may find that your story helps countless others, become a best-selling book and maybe abundance will follow. But the reason you chose to put your story out was to help others.

I was reading Richard Branson's book the other day and he was saying he always chose the options that represented the most fun for him. He was never chasing the money. As my husband says, if you chase money; money runs away. Branson loves to take risks. This is what he finds fun and enjoyable. He always made choices in his business based on what felt risky and fun for him.

For you, it might be different. Can you identify what lights you up? What makes you really happy or feel really comfortable. Start putting all this these ideas together and you begin to get a picture of what your ideal life would look like. Then start taking notice of the intuitive messages you receive, visualise your ideal life and one day, you may realise - 'Heck! I'm living my dream - I am a master manifester!"

Namaste!

Compiled by Kate Gardner

Wienke Ursula Schulenburg

Wienke Ursula Schulenburg works as a Life Coach, Psychologic Counsellor, Holistic Health Coach, Speaker and Author.

She is a living proof that it is totally possible to not only overcome trauma, but to turn misery into a mission and create a life full of joy, purpose and abundance. She is known for helping others create their own heart-centered business that reflects their deeper values and build avenues to giving their gifts to the world through writing and speaking.

Empowering others who have suffered from abuse, violence and traumatic experiences and help them find their truth, voice and identity is her sacred mission.

She has guided countless people to successfully turn their breakdowns into breakthroughs and take leadership in their lives and in the world.

soulcentered-evolution.com

Chapter 5

Coming from the soul…

By Wienke Ursula Schulenburg

The fact that you are here, holding this book in your hands, means that you already know so much and have come so far on your journey! And I am most probably not going to tell you anything new…

But may I invite you to have a profound *experience* of abundance, right here, right now? May I ask you to not just *read* this chapter, but to *feel* it – to *live* it? Together with me?

I could start by telling you a story of my life; where I was close to losing it all. Losing meaning: losing life. And I won't go into details here, but give you the essence straight away. When you are one step away of having to say goodbye, you are very clear about one thing: How much you actually have.

And your heart only desires one single thing: To be alive!

It is a simple and yet huge as that.

You don't think about bills, about a new car, about the lawn that needs mowing… You might not even think about your loved ones, because there is this inner knowing: I need to be alive *first* in order to care for them and be around for them. I *want* to be alive. You become aware of the preciousness of your being in a physical body. That it is the greatest gift you can experience and give to others: To be present.

Now, I don't believe we have to go through hardship or traumatic situations to come to this point. In fact, I realized, that we can have such profound experience at any given moment. At *any* given moment.

Without the threat of losing it all. Without the fear and anxiety.

It is about dying, yet not dying with the bad taste that usually comes with the word. It is about letting go. Letting it all go, until there is nothing but yourself. Your being alive. Can you do that?

Right now?

Letting go of the daily worries... right now... the bills yet to be paid, the argument with the boss... the conversation with your spouse and employee you will have... the business plan to be written, the phone call to make... Let it go and fade and come home to yourself. To your body. To your heart.

I invite you to place your hand over your chest while you are reading this and feel your breathing. Place on hand on your heart, feel its rhythm beneath your palm.

Come home. Be with your body, the physical expression of your life. Feel the aliveness... The warmth, the eagerness to live... The love for life and for yourself.

And if it feels good for you to do so, come one step further with me. Go deeper into this aliveness... Be it. With *all* that you are.

Can you feel the essence of yourself? Do you feel your soul, right here, shimmering through this aliveness? Can you see it reaching out to you, welcoming you home? Embracing you with so much love… Such deep, profound love…

Blend with this beautiful soul of yours. And look at your life, through the eyes of your soul. What do you see? Not with your mind, but with your soul?

What do you see?

You might see a deeper sense behind it all. An inner knowing that all is ultimately well. You will realize that those things that bothered you, actually don't matter. And that everything that comes from your soul, makes total sense.

You might realize, looking at your life, that there is only one thing you need to do, you would really *want* to do, which is to express the beauty and wisdom of your soul. To be a conductor for all you feel and experience right now. That bringing this gift to the world is the only thing that really matters. And doing it in the best way possible the only mission you have.

When we come from the soul life becomes so simple. Not because it is, but because we know our path. We know where to go. And we know it by the feeling of deep connection with our soul. It feels so right it couldn't be anything else. In these moments we know, with all our soul, that we are provided for. We know that we are being taken care of. There cannot be another possibility because we are on a sacred mission called our life and the whole universe, God, life itself is there to help us.

We feel that our soul, that we are, an individuation of this life force, being sent forth, wanting nothing more than going forth and express itself. It is impossible to fail. The doors are wide open for us to go out and live out what we know to be our truth, our mission, and our soul's agenda.

Now I would like to invite you to come back, into your body, into your physical aliveness. Feel the freshness, the eagerness to be alive. Feel the beauty of your heartbeat, of your breath.

Do you feel this overwhelm of love? Of gratefulness to be alive? To simply be? Maybe you are bathing in this knowing right now. Enjoy! Or maybe you are getting a glimpse of it, a gentle remembering of your inner truth. That is great!

We know that being alive is all we need to fulfill our divine agenda in this lifetime.

Being alive is all we need.

And there is so much aliveness within us, that we can barely embrace it. It is overflowing, pouring out of our soul into our body, into our life.

When we come from this place of richness there is nothing but gratitude we feel for this gift. And you don't have to survive a tragedy or wake up in the emergency room after having left your body to experience this, because *you* are allowing yourself to have this experience right here and right now.

You have just woken up and you are coming from your soul into your beautiful body, looking at your life and the next step you are going to take. The step that reflects your divinity, the step that expresses your soul's beauty and the step that fulfills your soul's agenda.

And yes, there are still the bills, the talk, and the work to do… But you look at it from a new and totally different perspective. You are coming from your soul and know where to go. And the distraction and voice of the mind that wants to keep us safe and alive, is no longer an obstacle, but just another force wanting to work *for us*. Our mind's worrying is, from this perspective, a demonstration of how much this part of us actually *loves* us, even demonstrating it in ways that do not always make things easier and serve us…

Our heart is expanded and we know with every cell of our body that life is having our back and that we are provided for. We are on a sacred mission and have come to do so with a strong partner to support us: with life itself.

So what is our soul's agenda? What are we to do, to be and to express?

It is not so much a concept, it is this inner knowing. This profound knowing, this deep feeling of being aligned, of being true to our mission. Of expressing our soul.

When we come from the soul, being in the high state of love and appreciation is our natural state of being. Our soul appreciates all there is. And blesses it.

When we come from this place we literally feel the cells of our body being so grateful for being alive. We feel deep appreciation for having this body that helps us do our work and participate in life. We are equipped with the perfect tool for our mission. We were provided for abundantly.

And when we get up and participate in life, we feel the inner compass, we feel the guidance, the connection to our soul. And overflowing with gratitude, all that life can do is to reflect back to us our inner state, showering us with possibilities, abundance and more experiences to be grateful for. All of a sudden we see the beauty and richness of life that has always been there, right in front of our eyes. We feel the friskiness of the air, see the warmth of a smile from a person we meet. We see the hand reaching out for us for help, so we may give our gift. We feel the heart that is beating and not only pumping blood through our blood vessels, but abundantly pumping love through us, reminding us that we are here for a reason.

We can use all those different wonderful tools to create the experience of abundance.

And we can go directly to our source. We can connect with our gift of being alive.

And we can do so by simply closing our eyes, placing one hand upon our chest and going within, gently dying a beautiful death, letting go of all we have hold on to, letting be all that we wanted to change. Leaving behind the world of our thoughts, the world of our daily tasks and connect with the essence of our body: The aliveness. And from there, already filled with gratitude, connecting with our soul and remembering *why* we chose this body, *why* we came to this world in the first place.

Remember this greater truth comes gently, as a silent feeling, a shimmer of inner light, growing bigger and bigger, filling us until there is no room for anything else and we feel strong enough to come back and approach life from this place of total abundance, purpose and security. Security because we are safe when we life our purpose. We are safe when we come from our souls.

There is no need to face death to remember our soul's agenda. We can die before we die, we can remember our truth at any given moment, we can connect with this inner source and let it's wisdom and abundance pour out through us.

When we come from our soul we are aligned. And when we are aligned things fall into place. They have to. They are the reflection of our inner state.

This experience has profoundly changed my life. Not once, but every time I go through it, it simplifies my life.

It helps to focus on what really matters. We cannot feel anything but gratitude when we are in contact with the total abundance and richness of being alive and having this body. This wonderful tool that enables us to walk on this planet and fulfill our soul`s agenda.

I hope this experience has touched you and reconnected you with what you already know, deep inside. And what every cell of your body is telling you, all the time, through its vibrational language.

Thank you for coming with me on this journey!

It holds the potential to transform your life.

Sylvia Friedman

For over 25 years, Sylvia Friedman has been changing people's lives - one TRUTH at a time.

As a motivational speaker, intuitive coach, handwriting analyst, astrologer and celebrated author, she not only sees the truth in others, she helps them discover it themselves. From the hallways of neighborhood housing projects, to the boardrooms of Chicago's top companies, to college classrooms and entertainment venues all around the world, Sylvia has guided individuals from all walks of life on a journey of self-awareness and acceptance with her signature blend of comedy, candor and compassion.

A graduate of Northwestern University's journalism and theatre programs, Sylvia has been featured on many media outlets, including *Oprah, Donohue, 190 North,* Lifetime, Fox, WGN, WLS and WJBC.

She is a recent recipient of an Inspired Award from *Today's Chicago Woman* magazine, and her book, **The Stars in Your Family: Relationships between Parents and Children** (Hay House), is in its 5th printing.

Visit Sylvia's website at www.sylviafriedman.com to view client comments and read how Sylvia has helped others find the TRUTH.

For private consultations, to schedule a workshop, entertainment or engage a powerful speaker/guest, contact Sylvia at 312-944-7256.

Chapter 6

Gratitude Feels Great!

By Sylvia Friedman

My father taught me to feel grateful for all of the good things that happened to me. I believe that my grateful nature saved my life. I was born in the Chicago Housing Projects, and lived there for the first twelve years of my life. I remained my parent's only child.

One would think that I would be lonely not having a brother or sister to grow up with, but I wasn't. I was happy to receive all of the love that my father gave me. I never felt poor, I never wanted more than I had, I didn't live with hate, and thought that everything I was given was a blessing. I felt abundant from the time I was little.

As I look back I know that my mother and me were not compatible. They say that you pick your parents, but I didn't think that I picked my mother. Somehow I knew that she was going to get in the way of my feeling grateful and abundant. I know that you may think that it's easier said than done, but my positive attitude helped me to know that if I belonged to myself and owned myself, I could believe in myself. I could not believe in myself if I allowed my mother to share her nervous and anxious behavior with me. My father told me that I was five years old when I said "I can't be like you mommy!" I could not communicate with my mother most of my life, although I think I loved her. I would always fear that her response was going to be "You're not good enough", as she was very judgmental and critical. Honesty was, and is still my best friend. Honesty and courage gave me the ability to be grateful, and even the smallest amount of joy made me feel abundant.

Growing up in the projects was a huge lesson, as it was considered a ghetto. As I observed all of my little friends' unhappiness, I knew I was lucky. I decided to become the leader of our group, and since my friends did not have much joy, living with their families, I thought it was my responsibility to bring it to them. I made up all kinds of games that we could play, and since I'm funny I would make them laugh. I felt abundant when I saw how much they loved me. I felt abundant when I could decrease their sadness. I felt abundance when I could save them. My friend Johnny's father was a Mafia person. I was playing in his house, which was very fancy. I loved to go there. One day I was going to the bathroom and saw his mother coming down the stairs, with blood all over her nightgown. I ran to look for Johnny's father, and he was in a meeting. I screamed, "Your wife is bleeding. You need to take her to the hospital. He looked at me as though he wanted to hit me, but he followed me to where his wife was. Johnny told me that I saved his mother, but his father said I couldn't play with him anymore. I was glad I could save his mother, and I was grateful that she did not die!

My father would ask me, "What makes you happy sweetheart?" I responded with "Love Is The Answer Daddy." I truthfully believe that my gratitude and abundance comes from all of the love I have received in my life.

I liked grammar school because it seemed easy, but there were times when I disliked it. I wasn't like the other kids in school, and there was one time when I had to deal with a "mean bully". She was very tall, and I was very short. My mother didn't dress me like the other kids, and I never had a pair of jeans. This girl, whose name was Natalie Klein would sit behind me every day. She would pull my hair, punch me in the stomach, and slap my face in the schoolyard. I went home and told my mother about Natalie, and asked her to come to school and see the principal. She was so frightened and said, "I can't go, and I'm sure that Natalie will stop hitting you." I was furious at my mother and decided to deal with Natalie myself.

We were out in the schoolyard and she came over to slap my face. I bent over and my head hit her in the stomach. She fell down and I slapped her face as many times as I could. Some kids told my teacher what I did and she took me to the principal. The principal asked, "Why did you fight with Natalie?" I answered, because she hit me every day and slapped my face. I wasn't going to let her do that anymore. The teacher asked, "Where is your mother?" I said, "She wouldn't come!" The teacher looked into my eyes and said, "You are a very brave little girl." She was the best teacher I ever had, and I was so grateful for her.

I skipped three times because they said I was very smart. I didn't like that because I had to go into high school at age 12. My parents were happy, because neither one of them was educated and they were very proud of me. There I was going into high school 30 lbs overweight. I made sure I lost the weight. I wasn't going to go to school "Fat and Young."

We moved out of the projects as I went into high school. The high schools in our neighborhood were not very good, and my parents knew that we had to move. We were still poor, but my uncle joined us so we could pay the rent. When I entered high school I wanted to find friends that were like me, because I knew that I wouldn't fit in with the popular kids. I was never bothered by being different, and I had an abundant amount of terrific friends, who stayed with me most of my life!

I graduated high school as valedictorian, and I was very grateful because my father was so proud of my accomplishment. I got into Northwestern University to study speech, drama, and journalism. I was definitely going to be an actress.

When I graduated high school I was off to New York City with my best friend Jean. Her father had a rich friend, who owned a building on east 64th and 2nd avenue. He said "I'll give them a studio for $50.00 a month. We were so happy that we would live in a fancy neighborhood, and split the rent. We still needed to get a job immediately. I was 19 and Jean was 21.

Fortunately we both got a job quickly. I had all of $150, and I *needed money*. I got a job working for the President of Transogram Corporation. I was the youngest one in the department, but luckily my boss liked me a lot. He was very considerate of me and if I had to come in late when I would audition for plays or commercials he never said a word. Talk about feeling grateful. The older women did not like me, but I didn't care. I was so happy in New York. I loved it. I was a rich young woman!

I used to go to the salvation army for clothes, since I didn't have a lot of money, and lo and behold I saw this fabulous coat. It was cashmere, with a leopard skin lining. It was only $40.00, and I couldn't wait to buy it. I didn't eat lunch for two weeks, but I had my coat. I was so happy.

This is the funniest story. After work I went to the corner store for a bottle of wine when I saw my friend Sam. I was wearing the coat without any clothes underneath. I loved the feel of the lining. It felt like my body was getting a massage. Sam took my arm and said, "We're having a party upstairs, come with me!" I responded with, "No, I'm just going to have a glass of wine and chips." He wouldn't take no for an answer and said, "You're coming with me" I thought to myself, as I was walking up the stairs to the party, "I have no clothes underneath this coat."

There I was sitting in the hot apartment, holding a glass of wine, and I couldn't take my coat off. My perspiration was getting all over my body. Finally, after two hours I said, "Sam, I'm going home." He responded with, "So Early!" I said, "Yes, I've gotta go."

Sam, looked at me for a moment and said, "You haven't taken off your coat!" I responded with, "I was cold." "COLD, he said." He started to laugh and said, "You don't have clothes underneath that coat!" I laughed and said, "No I don't!" I kissed him goodbye and went home to my apartment!.

Three years went by and my career in acting was going pretty well. One day my friend Sally called and said, "Lets go to this beach in Brooklyn. A lot of actors and dancers go there." I responded with, "I don't want to take a train to Brooklyn! After talking with her for an hour I was on my way to Brooklyn. I was lying down on my blanket, reading a script, when a young man was shaking keys over my head. He said, "Are these your keys? I found them three blankets down." He asked me to marry him at 4:30 pm that same day, and followed me everywhere. He was at the office, in front of my apartment building, and would not give up.

That's how I met my now ex-husband. I didn't want to get married to him or anyone else, as acting was going to be my life, but my journey included having my two beautiful children. To this day I am so grateful that God blessed me with my son and daughter. They are my true abundance.

We moved back to Chicago after we got married. I didn't want to, but I felt that I could see my father. I raised my children for the first 10 years of my life and then I went back to theatre. I spent 10 years on the stage, and my first standing ovation felt better than sex.

My husband earned a good living so we all lived well, but I was not happy in my marriage. I asked my husband for a divorce, beyond his objection, and I knew that my life would change. I had to get a job, because he hid all of our money, and we got very little. I got my first job as a producer, and I don't know how that happened. As I interviewed for the job I thought, "I don't know how I'm going to do this job, but I'll learn!" I must have made a good impression, because after a two hour interview, she said, "You are going to be my best producer." I worked with her for over seven years, and then she wanted to go back to New York. Of course I still needed to get another job, as my ex-husband wasn't giving us much money.

My girlfriend Vicky told me that she had a friend who needed a "Sports Agent"! I looked at her and said, "When can I interview?" She laughed out loud and said, "You don't know anything about sports!" I responded with my favorite thoughts "I don't know anything about sports, but I'll learn." I got the interview, and worked there for 4 years. I do not know how that worked for me, since I didn't know what a touchdown was. I had 50 yard line seats, and I would scream every time the Chicago Bears made a touchdown. My friends came with me, and explained all that was happening during the game. After a while I did very well.

I was so grateful for the jobs, as I needed to support my kids. They were always special, and contributed to the rent by getting jobs of their own. There it is again, gratitude and abundance.

I continued to act in the evening and met the love of my life. We spent twelve years together, and then the most horrible experience happened to me. I lost him and my father within three days. If I didn't build my self-love, and if I was not grateful for what I did have, I may have lost my mind. It took me three years to recover, but I made it through. I was very spiritual and believed that God always watched over me.

I decided to get another job, as a development director for the Heart Association. Again, I can do that, and if I can't I'll learn. I directed six divisions for 8 years and I loved it. I had a great boss, but directing the women's council, didn't work for me. They were very snobby, and I don't do well with fake personalities. My boss didn't want me to leave, but I thought it was time for me to start my own business.

I wanted to write a book about how Astrology affects children. I began to study Astrology, and wrote a book called "The Stars In Your Family" How to raise your kids as to who they are, rather than who you expect them to be!" It has become a bible for many families, and it was published in a month by Hay House. I felt so grateful, and my inner strength enhanced my abundance. I was so lucky.

I am now a speaker, An International Best Selling Author, Life coach, Astrologer, and Handwriting Analyst. Each day I learn something new, I don't feel rich, but I continue to feel abundant. Having a lot of money is not what makes me happy. I wouldn't be foolish enough to say that money isn't important, but what I do, and how I help people is what fulfills me. I am very grateful that I have this ability.

I teach Self-Love and a lot of people call me the Self-Love Guru. I know how it has worked for me all of my life. I know how much it has helped me in the worst of times. I know how it has increased my courage and inner strength. If an individual can hold on to valuing gratitude, and honoring their own self-love, they are rich, beyond compare.

Compiled by Kate Gardner

Lil Lezarre

Lil let her heart guide her and now she is living her life of dreams. She is a eight time best selling co-author, transformation guide, public speaker and has her own business which she started from scratch part time and now building into a franchise corporation. She has discovered her purpose and that's a motto she lives by – 'To encourage and inspire women's (& men's) fulfilment thru Respect, Honesty, Authenticity and Gratitude'. She is also developing programs to help people realize their purpose and start living their life of dreams. We all have abundance and the more you appreciate what abundance you have, the more you will receive.

www.lillezarre.com

Chapter 7

My Definition of Abundance

By Lil Lezarre

Funny how the first thing you think of when you think 'abundance' is lots of money or material possessions. Occasionally that still comes to mind but I know what the true definition of abundance is and I know because I've experienced it. It's abundance closer to a 'soul' level, meaning it's not the superficial one. It's the abundance you experience when you start realizing what a blessing it is to be you, to fill yourself up from the inside, to live life how it's meant to be lived, to gain true friendships.

I was raised in a religious and controlling family environment and at 16 ran away into another controlling relationship. 22 years later I ran away again but this time with my 3 children (then aged 4, 6 & 8). At the age of 38, it was the 1st time in my life that I started to experience true freedom. The freedom to be myself. I've been on this self discovery journey for 13 years now and the abundance I feel is beyond anything I ever would have dreamed of – ever. Here's my list:

Explore new activities

I've always had a love for our Canadian Rockies. When I had the freedom to take the kids and go as much as I wanted to, it gave me abundance on a whole new level. I'm not the 'high risk', like fast rides, kind of girl; I'm actually more of the close my eyes on the Farris wheel and afraid of heights kind of girl (literally to both of those). But, it turns out I love rock & ice climbing and skiing. If I have the urge to try it and if I like it, I can continue to do it. Now I regularly take groups of people to enjoy these activities in the mountains, introducing others to my passions gives me even more abundance.

Surround Yourself with only Positive and Supportive People.

I can honestly say that at this point in my life, I do not have one toxic person. There is no one that I cannot be honest with; Have to think about what I'm going to say before saying it so that it's not misconstrued; I wish I said something different in our conversations. It is awesome to have nothing but healthy relationships with supportive and authentic people. People you can sit back with and talk about anything and everything, as it comes into mind. I know what it's like to have a conversation where you're constantly thinking about what you're going to say before you say it because it's very important that it's perfect, if not, who knows what could happen. When you're in what I call the 'positive circle', everyone is here to support everyone; it's a 2-way street between every relationship. I know I can contact my best friends when I need help.

When it comes to business my mentors and coaches have been instrumental in helping me take my business to where it is today. Being an entrepreneur means you are your own walking billboard. Being authentic, confident, focussed, a leader, a good marketer attracts those same qualities and makes for amazing business relationships. I love what I do. My company is Tender Loving Cups. I started it from scratch in 2010 when I saw there was a need for ladies to find properly fittings bras at affordable prices. I change peoples lives. For you men out there, just think if your underwear cut into your balls – how important would the fit be then? Some ladies have just accepted it as fact, they can't find a proper fitting bra. Well I'm here to change that. I love the reactions I get: the hugs, the tears, the smiles, the 'Thank You'. I'm also a meditation teacher and the transformations I get to see right in front of me is so fulfilling. In 1 hour I see people go from stressed, tight faces to leaning back, eyes closed, totally relaxed everything, then a huge smile as they slowly open their eyes and stretch.

Kids

I have gone from having 3 kids (ages 4,6, & 8) 24 hrs / 7 days / week TO just me, at one point, every one of them decided to live with their dad. Those were some and of the hardest and lowest days of my life. My naturopath and counsellors were my best friends and I learned huge lessons during that hard time, like how to deal with loss and give myself permission to grieve. Now I have more abundance than I ever dreamed possible, all 3 kids are back in my life. I have an amazing relationship with all of them and they share my passion for the mountains and activities in them. I've also developed a program for the parent going through a divorce and is trying to do the right thing, not use the kids and not badmouth the ex. I've been there and survived and now I share my tools with the world. We go through the hard times to grow and learn lessons. I wouldn't change anything about my past, it's all made me who I am today and I love being me.

We all have so much abundance; it's about what's important to us and knowing we can get it and willing to work for it. I feel great inside with an overflow of abundance. It's taken a lot of work to get me here and I'm definitely reaping the benefits on many dimensions. I am loving life, everything about it. That's abundance.

Emma Coker

To date I have spent 20 years working with individuals across the globe to attract and coach talented well beings. My holistic approach enables individuals and companies to work from a mind, body and spirited way in their everyday working lives. I assist clients to achieve personal and professional goals that are not born out of stress. I have a first class degree in life and a passion for excellence when it comes to seeing my clients find their wings and soar to the heights they set themselves.

Life is too short to not live it in a passionate and compelling fashion because even though a storm may arise there will ultimately be a rainbow.

Find out more at:

www.emmajoelcoker.com

Chapter 8

The Princess and The Bentley

By Emma Coker

I picked 3 dresses. I know me in a dress...but you had to wait until you were dead for that to happen. I chose well, and even though you spent most of my childhood and most of my life living all over the world, I wanted you to have a very British funeral. I chose red, white and blue. Vivienne Westwood and a big red hat.

Joery (The son my father never really had) arrived from Belgium. On the way back from the airport, the first song on the radio was John Secada," Just Another Day". Joery leapt forward and said, "It's your song Emma!" "The one you left for your Dad in Curacao". I didn't know he knew. I was choked, I was honoured and I cried.

The service was tough. I read, I cried, I sang, and then a great big bloody ex-military plane flew across the big window of the crematorium. You couldn't help yourself could you? You had to gate crash my big moment you bugger! However, I was ever so grateful for the sign that you approved of the service I had arranged. Nice one Dad!

I had ordered a cab, as the wake was coming to an end. I was tired, we were all tired but 'He' was not in the best of moods. It started with a push, then a shove, and before I knew it, I was down on the ground. His grubby hands were around my throat again. This time it felt different, this time people watched. This time people shouted, and thankfully came to my rescue; as on previous occasions, he had done it in the privacy of my own home.

I was carried back to the pub where we held your wake, the landlord closed the doors and curtains, and I sat there in the blur of what had just happened. With my head in my hands I prayed, "Dear God, on the day of my Father's funeral, of all the days to pick, why did 'He' pick this one?"

The following morning the phone rang. I answered, it was my husband ringing to get an update on the sale of the house. Although we had separated, we still had assets to break and he seemed relentless in his breaking of mine. How long does it take? Your Father died 3 months ago, surely you must have dealt with it all by now? Those were his words, and I was dumb struck. I didn't realise grief had a timeline, but apparently, when it comes to releasing your soon to be ex-husband from the mortgage, there is.

I opened the post and there it was in black and white, the court order initiating the forced sale of my home. I opened the next piece of post and there it was in black and white, the operation date for my emergency hysterectomy. There is no such thing as an emergency hysterectomy, even when you need one. So you have to book it and wait, even though you feel like death, and you pray it will come soon.

I boarded the boat for Holland and drove while under the influence of several varieties of painkillers. I couldn't wait to see her, the Mason Black Beauty. I was finally bringing her home. The Bentley was going to be in the hands of your daughter and I was going to cherish every single moment of the drive back home. She, the Bentley, was your dying wish, and we bought her together, do you remember? She arrived on December 28th and we smiled. Even though you were very frail, you insisted on driving her back to Holland.

I was mortified when customs stopped you and you missed your slot to board the boat. You had to see the cancer surgeon so early and you hardly got any sleep. I should have come with you, but alas, 'He' made me feel guilty. Made me feel guilty for wanting to spend so much time with you in those precious hours we were given just after you were diagnosed.

I wanted to park her on the driveway at home. 'He' wanted her parked at our workshop on the farm. I protested, and again I woke up with more bruises.

His appendix burst just after your funeral, and he nearly died. I nursed him back to health, delayed my own surgery and buried my grief.

The court set a hearing date for the forced sale of my home, and I began to sell everything I could to pay for Christmas. 'He' watched, did nothing and rolled another cigarette.

My solicitor agreed and said he should leave, probably best if I don't live with a man, as my ex-husband could charge him rent. Irony really, as neither of them ever contributed a penny, and yet both of them were about to take me for everything I owned. I didn't realise they would take my dignity as well.

My Big Operation was successful and I was pain free for the first time in 20 years. It was a bitter pill at 42 to know I would not have a legacy of Coker's but you were gone now, so I assumed you didn't mind.

I healed quickly, and within 2 weeks I was packing up my home. The court had decided I didn't deserve my home, and had agreed the forced sale in favour of my soon to be ex-husband. I couldn't afford to live there anymore, and I couldn't afford the emotional cost either.

I drew a bath and got on the scales, 8 stone 4lbs. Wow! how did that happen? I was 10 stone 2lbs on an average day.

At 5pm, I walked along the towpath. It was my birthday, and 'He' had promised me dinner. I had brought the last pieces of my birthday cake to share. He knew I loved my birthday, and met me in a canoe, paddled me all the way to his canal boat. You know, the one you suggested I pay for, clear his mortgage with monies you had left me? So I did, not sure why I did, and not sure why you asked me to either, but all the same, I did.

That night 'He' told me I was a princess, told me that you treated me like a princess, and in hindsight, I should have kept the Bentley and not sent her to auction as 'He' had originally suggested. How could I? All my cash had gone and he wasn't about to get a job and pay the bills.

I cried. I hated crying on my birthday, as I always believe it brings bad luck.

It did!

At 5.30 am, I sent the following text: "Hi, I got beaten up last night, can you ring me as soon as you wake up please, I really need a friend." I had hidden my car a mile away from where I was living, ran a salt bath and sat in it, with the lights off all night. I was terrified he would come and find me and do it all again. I was broken, bruised, and humiliated.

The police and the hospital treated me like a broken sparrow. My best friend cried as I stood half naked being gently assessed by the medical team. Her youngest daughter didn't leave my side and her husband was a tower of strength. I gave my statement, had 17 photographs taken and wept like a small child.

Within 3 days I was back in Sunbury with a few bags, a broken spirit, but a heart full of hope. I was back in the village were you and Mum brought me up. I bumped into familiar faces and I began to feel safe. It was home.

I began to eat. It was slow and it was hard, but over time my weight began to creep up. I didn't look like a former shadow of myself, and I was beginning to heal.

The phone rang and I was overjoyed. The job! I got the job, and now I can find a place to live.

I was grateful to have lived at my Mum and Stepfather's home, but I couldn't heal as quick because I couldn't help but feel I was in the way. I hadn't lived at home for years, and My Mum and Stepfather continued to insist that I wasn't in the way, but I wanted to talk about my Dad. It wasn't a popular subject. My parents didn't part on the best of terms, and Mum couldn't really understand how I nursed the man that left me at age 7. I didn't argue and I understood her point of view, but all I wanted to do was heal.

A week later, I met the rental agent at the foot of the stairs. I opened the door, took 3 steps in and smiled. The Penthouse. Wow dear god! Thank you; I am going to live in a penthouse.

The alarm went off at 4am as it did every Monday. I showered, dressed, and headed for the taxi. I worked in Paris – oh my god did you hear me! - I worked in Paris.

It took 18 months of hell, it was very real, and it was very, very harsh. I lost my home, my father, my dignity, and every last breath to find my smile, but I did it. I did it. I got up, dusted myself down and became your daughter once more Mum and Dad.

You taught me to fight, to dream, and to never give in even when you did. You taught me to hold my knife and fork properly, to speak well and to educate myself. You told me to fly around the world, to holiday on my own, and to learn to like my own company. Dad said, "Eating is cheating and sleep is for losers." Thankfully I didn't take that advice too often. Mum said, "Chin up and face forward darling" and I still do that even on my most difficult days.

I eat, I sleep, and I educate myself. I speak well, I still hold my knife and fork properly, and I really enjoy my own company.

My future gets brighter every day and I have my dignity back. I don't have you Dad, but I do have Mum, my stepfather John, my sister Kelly, and a head full of amazing memories.

Without my back story, I wouldn't be writing this chapter. Without the pain, there would be no gain. Without yesterday, there would be no tomorrow.

I am eternally grateful for all that I have experienced and accomplished, and yes, even those very harsh times.

To My Father, I would simply say: "Dad, it's been a rollercoaster since you have been gone, but I still have Mr Blue Sky. Although we only had a few weeks together before you passed, I am blessed and grateful that we did.

Mum, I know I drive you insane most days with my never ending search for the pot of gold at the end of the rainbow, but I know deep down you are grateful for my animated stories and adventures.

Dear and very patient Stepfather (John), you are a saint. I don't need to say anymore. You are always there to catch my fall and I am grateful that I know how to wrap the cheese properly before putting it back in the fridge.

Kelly, my sister, we continue to grow as Sisters every day, and I am grateful for our crazy 500miles an hour phone conversations.

Gratitude comes in many ways, and not always in the box or the coloured wrapping you expect. I didn't expect my gratitude to come in the form of an abusive relationship, a failed marriage, a complete wipe out financially, or as a consequence of not being able to bare children, but it did.

Today as I write this chapter, I am happy, healthy, and facing forward. I have a future that is rosy and second to none, and I will always search for that pot of gold at the end of the rainbow.

The Princess and The Bentley

Jeff Hutchens

Jeff Hutchens is a graduate of The Coaching Academy with over seven years' experience in coaching, and is an NLP Practitioner. Jeff, the 'Stress-less Coach', is based in the South West of England, and he is the author of four books: 'Take Back Control: coach yourself to a stress-less life', 'Take Back your Confidence', 'Take Back your Mountain: Success and reflection from Everest Base Camp', and 'The Coaching Calendar: daily inspiration from the stress-less coach'.

Jeff has a passion for helping people unlock their confident selves to live a stress-less life and passionately pursue their dreams.

For more information on Jeff please visit

www.thestresslesslife.co.uk

Chapter 9
Gratitude for abundance –
The Time Traveller's Life
By Jeff Hutchens

Sometimes on this journey of life, you just have to stop and take time out for yourself, so that you can reflect on all that you have, or have had in the past, and even what you will have in the future. It is time to take a look around, and start paying attention, and realise exactly what you do have and notice how blessed you are; to see just how much abundance there is all around you – you have been given so much to bless you. In some ways, when you choose to have an attitude of gratitude it is a little like time travel, it allows you to stop and look back, delve into your past, and realise how much you have been given, how much you had, and how much there is in your life. It lets you see that there is so much that you can appreciate, if you just take the time to look around you and realise how fortunate and how blessed you are.

Like many people, judging by the film and television industry, I am fascinated by the idea of time travel. I have enlightened many with my wild and whacky theories about the relativity of time...don't ask!! But I think that gratitude is an amazing way to stop, expand, and travel back and forth in time – as you seek to see the world with eyes of appreciation and wonder. Delving back into beautiful times, good times, places you have been, people you have known, friendships you have had, relationships you have had, family members you have loved and lost, and those still in your life. There is so much that you do have in your life, the people in your life who bless you every day, the people who bless you just once and then move on, people who have loved you, given into your life, cared for you, the things you have in your life, places you have around you, places you have been, places you will go as you set goals and think into the future as you look forward in time. There is so much of the world around you to be grateful for. Gratitude takes time…expands time… It lets you travel in time, into the past, and on into the future…It's important in life to take some time out – make time stop for you – and use the time to reflect… to work out exactly what and who you can be grateful for.

You can always be grateful for the people in your life; past, present, and future. Family members who took their time to bless you, and I have amazing memories of parents and grandparents who made time for me, along with a lovely sister, and fabulous brother to share those times with, alongside extended family. Occasions and holidays where we spent so much quality time, and if I let myself by taking the time, I am back there in an instant as I reflect with gratitude. It is like I have travelled back in time as I enjoy the blessing once again with a grateful heart. Friends too; through school, work, church, and on tour with my mime troupes – travelling through various parts of the world. There are my university friends, and those special friends into the present time. When I take the time to relive memories, past and into the present, it is the life of the time traveller in gratitude; so much abundance that carries no monetary value but is measured in precious moments of life.

At present in particular, I am so grateful for my fabulous daughter, who recently had an amazing time on holiday creating new memories that are all part of the time we spend together that I am so thankful for. I know there would be times that I will look back on again in future with an attitude of gratitude for such an amazing small person in my life who teaches me so much.

Life is not all sunshine and roses, and I'm sure that you have had good experiences and experiences which seemed bad for you at the time, but turned out to be a 'blessing in disguise'. Have a think about the person that you are now, and reflect on what has contributed to make you who you are: maybe something fabulous, maybe something tough which made you stronger or something difficult which has taught patience and perseverance. These are strong qualities which you would not have had after all: the strongest steel is borne of the blast furnace…all of these things are fuel for your gratitude.

It may be that like me, events cause you to stop and take stock of your life…they give you the impetus to pause and reflect, and allow yourself appreciate what you have. The death of my lovely sister has allowed me take time out to remember so many fabulous times… to time travel back and relive some of those precious memories to truly appreciate what a fabulous sister she was, and to appreciate the very many good times that we shared. Wandering down Rose Street in Edinburgh this summer, I was suddenly reminded of times with her, and bitter/sweet memories of her, and sense of her lovely presence, and a joy to be in a place that was one of her favourites. Once I stopped to think, I realised that there was so much joy in the pain, and I was reminded of the words of CS Lewis in the movie 'Shadowlands' as he dealt with the certain death of his wife to cancer. He stated that 'the joy now is part of the pain then' and once she had passed away he returned to his thoughts to flip the phrase to realise that 'the pain now is part of the joy then'… I love this, as it is pure time travel gratitude… linking the pain he was experiencing with the joy of his wife when she was around, it allows me remember that the strong pain felt now for the loss of my sister is linked strongly to the joy I had with her when she was alive, and the memories that I can experience have that bitter/sweet quality of pain for her passing, but joy and gratitude for the times when she was here. Even in the pain there is a reason to be grateful, there is so much in life to be grateful for when time is taken just to realise what you have or had. It is only in gratitude that we can make sense of any loss in our lives… and there is so much to appreciate when we time travel in gratitude for the people who have so enriched our lives.

As for the future… how do we time travel forwards in gratitude? If you let yourself, you can look forward into your future with an attitude of gratitude, ready to look for and embrace the abundance that the world has to offer. This is about looking for opportunities to be grateful for what comes your way, ready to thank those who cross your path as you look for the positive in all areas of your life. This is a choice that is always available to you, as you time travel into a future with gratitude for the amazing things that will come into your life, for the incredible places you will go, and the people who are in your life now and who will enter your life in your abundant future… because you can always choose your attitude each day.

I recently read the following on Facebook: 'To be happy you must: let go of what is gone, be grateful for what remains, and look forward to what is coming next' from a group called "the power of positivity", and it encapsulates much of what I believe regarding happiness, gratitude, and abundance. It is all about the choices you make in your life. Every experience of life has some reason to be grateful – but we have to choose to look for it, and open up to the feelings of abundance that it reveals for us. We can always choose our response, and we can always choose gratitude. We can always choose to time travel, to stop time, and to future proof ourselves with an attitude that is grateful for the past, appreciative in the present, and looking out for what we can be thankful for in the future. Gratitude makes sense of our lives as we realise the amazing abundance all around us in this amazing world we have been given. How will you choose to live? Will you choose to be a time traveller in gratitude? Will you choose a life of abundance?

Compiled by Kate Gardner

Laurie Vallas

Laurie is inspired by the little things in life – and has started to share them in a bigger way through writing. She doesn't claim to have mastered all of the lessons life has to offer, and therefore remains open and curious to the littlest of clues; continuously exploring under every rock for more. What Laurie is most known for is the contagious 'heart-sighting' movement she has begun among her circle.

An artist, advocate, and Founder of The Heartifacts; the business of facilitating the discovery, excavation, and transformation of untapped value – she is committed to, and passionate about getting to the heart of all that matters.

Laurie currently lives in the US with her husband Larry and their two cats Wilson and Fiona; but considers her home – naturally, where her heart is.

You can reach Laurie at:

Website: www.theheartifacts.com/

Email: theheartifacts@gmail.com

LinkedIn: Laurie Vallas

Facebook: Laurie Vallas – Author, The Heartifacts *and* PositiviTEAs

Twitter: @TheHeartifacts

Chapter 10

The Glocalization of Gratitude & Greater Goodness

By Laurie Vallas

As I stood in the shower one morning, I realized how easily I am drawn into spontaneously and sometimes recklessly spending money on the latest hair and skin care products.

Then I began to ponder how funny it was that most of my creative inspiration comes whilst in the shower; although this is not unusual for most creative types. The musing continued as I considered the possible correlation between the great writers of Ireland, England, Scotland, and Wales – and all of that rain.

I went back to thinking about the half-used bottles – how I am constantly sampling a wide variety of products... how easily I become distracted by the latest-and-greatest ones – until my attention turned towards how the surplus of all this great, yet half-used goodness had also become ridiculously overwhelming. That wasn't good at all.

While the water continued to flow, the mindless pondering continued – until a sobering awareness began to emerge of how arrogant and irresponsible I was to allow all this inspiration to cascade freely as I also carelessly let all that clean water run down the drain.

Indulgent mindfulness quickly turned into an uncomfortable alarm as I began to realize just how fortunate I am; that not only did I have the luxury of a clean, warm shower – but that both my time, and the idleness of standing in the shower was perceived as unlimited. Guilt over the excessive products was now secondary.

I quickly bolted from the shower – flustered by the possibility of what is so casually disposable for me – in all its reckless frivolity – could be equated to setting fire to $1m dollars or pouring gold down a drain. I felt ill – and selfish.

How could this happen?

My father recycled before it was trendy and my mother grew up in poverty – so messages of frugality, repurposing and gratitude for what we have were not new subjects to me.

So how could I have strayed so far? More concerning to me was – why?

I grew up appreciating old things – and history. Both contain great stories. As a young teenager, I spent my Saturday afternoons independently roaming around local antique shops getting to know the owners and admiring all of the old, fantastic objects. I lived in an historic neighbourhood – and the house I grew up in was built in circa 1820. It was always under some sort of restoration and I remember watching my father peel away layers off the walls in need of repair. Quietly, I marvelled with fascination at the horse-hair plaster and square-tipped nails that held the aged, yet sturdy bones of my old house together.

Our current home is over a century old. Because I love old things, I see and appreciate the beauty and value of what was. Gathering around the table and listening to the myriad of stories that make up my combined family's history is something I cherish. For most of us, feelings of appreciation frequently come after it's too late to express them. The comedians, sages and storytellers of my family will be gone one day – and I have experienced enough sudden loss to conclude that I refuse to be stunned with regret and consequently shocked into gratitude. I now whisper to myself;

'Let life inspire your gratitude – not death'

Perhaps this is an odd way to begin a conversation about Gratitude, but it is relevant.

You may be curious about how these three themes of waste, history and death could inspire me – or anyone – to feel abundant every day; how these categories serve as roots to how I came to define Gratitude, and how I believe that an examination of what is great amidst the minutiae of our daily lives can have a greater and more positive global impact.

I found that greatness is often embedded in the details.

"Like a lotus flower that grows out of the mud, and blossoms above the muddy water surface, we can rise above our defilements and sufferings of life."

~ Buddhist Saying

Speaking of rising above muddy waters; despite the risks to our mental health and overall well-being, my husband and I watch the news nearly every single night. My rationale is that this keeps me aware of what kind of negativity I could encounter during the next day. My husband often concludes, "Greed is ultimately the root cause of all of humanity's problems." Sadly, I believe this may be accurate.

I began to wonder; why does it seem the average person could have everything they want – focus on getting it – and in the end, quickly lose the connection to the joy they were certain to feel post-acquisition, ending up not really wanting what they thought they wanted?

Did 'it' lose value? If so, how so?

Is 'it' not 'great' anymore? If not, why? What changed – if anything?

How can these two perspectives come together to arrive at a sense of Gratitude? The way I see it, it's more difficult to get to a mind and heart-set of 'everything is full of greatness' unless what is 'not so great' is also examined. However the real inhibitor to the conversation is the focus within 'either/ or – great/ not great' parameters. Subsequently, so much energy is invested in defending one perspective to the other. And the reality is this:

> *"People who wonder whether the glass is half empty or half full miss the point.*
>
> *The glass is refillable."*
>
> ~ Unknown

I believe integrating the concept and practice of Gratitude, combined with the awareness of a greater goodness – both locally and extended globally, can be achieved in a cumulative series of tiny ways; beginning with the awareness that all life, particularly yours, is actually ***full of greatness***.

I've noticed when people struggle to acknowledge and embrace their greatness – they sometimes unwittingly attempt to hinder, extinguish or obstruct another's. I believe this occurs when people fear they will be left behind – or worse, left out. The truth is – there is an abundance of kindness and goodness available and the world will never run out of it. The glass will always expand to hold it all. We cannot let the fear of lack win.

There is an increased focus on science of mind research, suggesting that the quality of one's life improves significantly by embracing an 'Attitude of Gratitude'.

Achieving this requires a daily practice. I've not mastered it yet, but I began testing this concept by carefully examining smaller, ordinary events until I was able to transfer this philosophy to bigger, more significant aspects of my life.

Let me illustrate how I developed this theory by sharing a little technique I often play with:

- Pause for a moment to realize how great it is that you are able to read this.
- Now, grateful for your eyesight – are you wearing glasses?
- If so, think about how this is even more of a reason to feel grateful because it means you either have the means to buy glasses and/or insurance to help pay for them.
- If you have insurance to help support this need, and other healthcare – it is likely you also have a job. Now let's stretch this a bit more…
- If you have a job – how great is it that you have good health that enables you to get to work every day (and also that you have a job to go to every day)
- If you drive to work, feeling grateful for that car and how great it is that there were people whose creativity shaped the industry in which you work; that it provided so much opportunity for so many people that an office building needed to be built – creating even more jobs for people. Also in this mix of great stuff is that there were also inventors of cars, labourers who – literally – paved the way for us to get from one place to another…

And the list could go on.

"When you eat fruit, think of the person who planted the tree"

~ Vietnamese Saying

How was that exercise? Have you ever thought of your life in that way or at that level of detail before? Have you ever become so present to the wide variety of tiny particulars that are, in reality, enormously great contributions that incrementally provided a greater quality to your life? Broken down in this way, it's easier to see that greatness is everywhere, and the world as being full of greatness. Therefore, being 'great-full' requires mainly awareness.

Armed with this new outlook; how does this idea of, 'the world is full of greatness' sound? How does this sentence make you feel?

When it comes to Gratitude, I feel people are generally aware of the concept; we know – theoretically – why it's important – why it's an important behaviour – why it's good for us, and why it has so many positive aspects to our physical, mental, emotional, and spiritual well-being in all areas of our lives.

But, do we **understand** why Gratitude is a critical component to manifesting all of our heart's desires?

Awareness of every single aspect of our lives and cognizance of everywhere and everything we could possibly be grateful for within those realms could result in:

- An easing of anxiety and depression to support a healthier immune system
- Helping us 'bounce back' from difficult events
- Creating more meaningful relationships inspired by both forgiveness and kindness
- Greater respect for ourselves and for others
- Better quality of sleep
- Spontaneous surges of happiness – igniting that 'spring in your step'
- Sharing smiles and thank-you's – acknowledging that others are seen and worthy
- Energy to volunteer; becoming the groundwork for building stronger communities
- Deep joy – the kind that comes when your heart's deepest wishes are fulfilled
- Miracles... lots of them

My question is: if an attitude of gratitude is so good for us and everyone around us, why is it so difficult to sustain?

I've reached the conclusion that it's the chronic bombardment of negative, inaccurate messages emanating primarily from the mainstream media is a significant obstacle to seeing the greater goodness and a threat to happiness. We all ask ourselves, "Why is it that the news is always focused on what's negative?" My father has often responded to my lament with, "...for some time now, the media is no longer content with simply reporting the news;

the industry now feels obligated to create it." What I want to know is why aren't we asking ourselves, "…how can we elevate our behaviour so that there is nothing negative to report?"

While I continue to watch the news, I am testing out a simple philosophy, mantra and strategy to transform and strengthen my own vulnerability to negative programming:

"Promote what you love with so much passion it eradicates all apathetic indifference"

My efforts are supported tremendously by watching *Sunday Morning with Charles Osgood* every week with my mother. We ring each other during the commercials to share and compare reflections. If it weren't for those cherished 90 minutes of positivity, I'd most certainly have a hard time facing the week ahead.

Through this weekly ritual, I've realized that primarily reading and sharing positive stories over reading and sharing negative ones is a way to become my own local reporter. If people are unsure how to promote good stories in the midst of so many bad ones – then encourage them to make sure they are part of a good one. If everyone – literally everyone unplugged from negative media sources, became aware that our behaviour is the powerful and influential antidote, then I am certain there would be a global shift in mind and heart-set.

This way of looking at gratefulness, what's full-of-greatness and gratitude can be contagious; hold the door for someone, smile at strangers or let someone go ahead of you in traffic –

kindness and respect as gestures of gratitude can be assimilated into our lives just as easily as all the other 'unmentionable' stuff in the media circuits can.

I believe that the awareness of greatness is diluted when our focus is distracted towards what's –

- …wrong
- …to be feared
- …to be bought
- …to 'get' better
- …to be done faster

Gandhi was right, "There's more to life than increasing its speed."

We are moving so fast through our days that we may not even notice the subtle, slow-creeping negative influences – and how could we?

This speeding means the lines between momentum and evolution can become blurred – which I feel contributes towards distorting the distinction between reality and perception.

My father often says, "Progress means change – however change does not always mean progress." I wonder: How could I have succumbed to the habit of believing that more – or new – was better?

Don't get me wrong – new is necessary. New ideas, perspectives, and research are all important, if not vital.

Items, as well as some ideas, eventually wear out and are used up, and an opportunity to replace them is healthy.

The suggestions, thoughts and ideas I've shared are not new concepts, but rather – renewed, repurposed and even recycled ones.

You either purchased this book for yourself, or received it as a gift. You're reading it because you're curious, open, seeking inspiration – or a combination of these.

No one has all the answers, but all of us have some of them. Everyone is trying to navigate their way through life and in their own way wanting to discover a sustainable and reliable pathway to happiness. Sharing our experiences, challenges and successes is the most generous way to shed light over another's compass. As Edith Wharton said,

"There are two ways of spreading light; to be the candle or the mirror that reflects it."

These perspectives are invitations to shed light on life's events; to be aware of the next time we lose sight and cannot distinguish between what no longer has meaning to us versus what are actually symptoms of boredom, and therefore lack of effort. This pertains to all of our relationships, too.

Not seeing the greatness or the goodness in sustainable ways in all areas of our lives can lead to taking things and people for granted. The belief that we can always get another can slowly become a habit. This becomes particularly interesting in the health department – as it's all too common (myself included) to slip into a habit of taking our bodies for granted. There is a huge emphasis to have a plan for Wealth Management; but do we consider a serious plan for 'Wellth Management'? Awareness is a large percentage of solutions.

Still, there are so many aspects to life where seeing the greatness everywhere and in every aspect of life – nature, animals, etc. included on a local level would certainly begin to turn the lens on animosity – would you agree?

If attention was focused on the greatness of people, respect for them would follow more naturally. These seedlings of local change can gradually have a positive global impact. Or, as a colleague recently defined it to me as, "Glocalization" – a contemporary word that summarizes the 1970's phrase, 'Think Globally, Act Locally'.

Let's explore this theory a bit and think about all of the things that could potentially improve at a global level if we looked at Gratitude in a global 'Wellth Management' context:

- All would be fed and nourished
- Water would be available, clean and accessible
- There would be humane and dignified shelter
- Information and knowledge would be shared versus hoarded
- Poverty would be eradicated

- Our natural environment would be improved – protecting animals and their habitats
- Greater collaboration to combat disease
- Resources would be pooled
- Violence in all forms would come to an end
- War would be part of history's past

Visualize this wellness flowchart: Where there is relevance – there is value. Where there is value – there is worthiness. Where there is worthiness – there is respect. Where there is respect – there is happiness. Where there is happiness – there is peace. Where there is peace – there is kindness…

Gratitude is defined as, 'The quality of being thankful, readiness to show appreciation for, and to return kindness.'

Believe you are full of greatness. Risk believing in the greater goodness of others and how that can expand your capacity for kindness. Believe that because of your kindness locally, you contribute to inspiring kindness in areas of the world you may never visit. Consider believing that perhaps the kindness extended to you originated from that place and is now merely coming back to you.

Now for some homework: Today I will share my greatness by_____ *(fill in your own action)*

Are you ready to feel abundantly grateful every day?

Who knows, perhaps a (modest) morning shower may inspire your thoughts of changing the world, too…

Compiled by Kate Gardner

Stephanie J. Alvarez

Stephanie J. Alvarez is first and foremost a mother to a beautiful girl named Angelina De Amor Alvarez and an adorable Maltese named Mr. Furly. Stephanie and her brother Jesse were raised by their mother Lydia in a single parent home. Stephanie hated seeing her mom work so hard while living check to check. Stephanie always had a vision of retiring her mom and helping millions of families like hers become financially free when she grew up.

Stephanie J. Alvarez is a philanthropist / humanitarian. Stephanie volunteers as the Program Manager for CHOICES, which is a workshop that empowers teens to achieve academic success in pursuit of their career and life aspirations. Stephanie also volunteers her time with many other organizations in the community that teach financial literacy. Stephanie serves on the Board of Directors as the Treasurer for the Discovery Bay Community Foundation.

Stephanie J. Alvarez, an eleven-year financial industry veteran, is a Certified Financial Education Instructor, Certified Identity Theft Risk Management Specialist, Real Estate Salesperson, and Licensed Life & Health Insurance agent. Stephanie J. Alvarez is the founder of UMPH INC. (est. 2014), an international financial education and services firm. Stephanie is also a lightworker. She uses her energy work on clients who want help breaking through the blocks preventing them from achieving financial freedom.

Stephanie J. Alvarez is a member of the Personal Finance Speakers Association. Stephanie believes that a strong financial education is the best investor asset, and is passionate about teaching others the strategies and tactics used to become financially free.

Connect with me at

www.linkedin.com/in/stephaniejalvarez

www.facebook.com/theoriginalstephaniejalvarez

stephaniejalvarez@gmail.com

www.umphinc.com

408-509-9455

Chapter 11

Manifest Abundance Using Gratitude

By Stephanie J. Alvarez

Many years ago, my brother Jesse tore both of his patellar tendons while playing basketball. He did a pump fake and when he came down, the years of playing competitive sports was too much for his tendons to handle. He did not know the severity of the injury at the time. He asked his buddies to roll him under the basketball hoop thinking he just needed to take it easy. When he tried to get up, he saw his kneecaps coming up to his middle thigh. He then asked his buddies to help him sit on the bench off to the side. After a while he tried to get up again and the same thing happened. At this point he knew something was really wrong and he called an ambulance. When the paramedics came, they did a brief intake and put him on a sturdy blanket to lift him onto the gurney.

When they lifted him his knees bent down and his kneecaps slid to his thigh again. One of the paramedics whispered to the other "did you see that?" My brother grew more concerned after hearing this. When they arrived at the hospital, the Dr. said the only other time he had seen this was from a car accident. Jesse was bedridden and non-weight bearing for 4 months. A once very active athlete and bodybuilder, was now down and out for the count. My mom took some time off of work to help him during this time. I was working from home at the time, so I also was able to help out. My mom had to wash his hair in the sink, and he only got to wipe himself down with a cloth and some soap. He had to learn to transfer from his bed to the wheelchair where his legs were always at a 90-degree angle. He was not able to go outside for months because it was too difficult for us to get him outside with his wheelchair. He was a Realtor, and also just starting a new business when this happened, and it destroyed his livelihood. After 4 months of no walking at all and no real bath, he had to have another surgery to remove the wire that was put in place to stabilize his knee. This time he was down for another month. Finally after 5 months of no walking, he began 6 months of rehab to learn to walk again. It was a slow and painful process for him, but his competitive spirit kept him going.

Jesse is a pretty positive person, this runs in our family, and he used the power of gratitude to change things around. I remember how happy and grateful he was when he was able to take a real shower. Once he was able to get back on his feet and begin working again, he was so grateful for all of the little things that he began to attract abundance in all forms into his life. His heart was filled with gratitude, which caused his health and finances to improve rapidly. Jesse is currently in the best shape of his life since High School, and his business is flourishing.

I believe the power of the feeling of gratitude is one of the most powerful tools we have to attract abundance into all areas of our lives. Every morning I wake up, the first thing I do is think of all of the things I am grateful for in my life. Every time something big or small happens in my favor during the day, I say, "thank you". Sometimes I even do a little dance to get the feeling moving through my whole body.

When I hear my clients beating themselves up about not starting a financial freedom plan sooner or being in debt, I remind them about all of the things they have to be grateful for. I tell them to be grateful for taking the first step. I remind them of where they will be in a year from now, 5 years from now, and so on. I also let them know the importance of their attitude when we work together, to ensure a positive outcome. I encourage them to use the power of feeling grateful to transform their financial status.

I have random gratitude lists that I have kept throughout the years, and from time to time, I will find one and reflect on the things I listed. I immediately remember how good I felt when I wrote the list. I tend to be my own worst critic, and it is really nice to be reminded of my victories and all the things that happened to bring me to where I am currently.

In her popular book *The Secret*, Rhonda Byrne writes, "With all that I have read and all that I have experienced in my own life, using *The Secret*, the power of gratitude, stands above everything else. If you do only one thing with the knowledge of the book, use gratitude until it becomes your way of life."

Wikipedia defines gratitude as a feeling or attitude in acknowledgment of a benefit that one has received or will receive. I believe the missing piece in gratitude is the FEELING. Most people just go through the motions when they are making a gratitude list or thinking about the things they are grateful for.

Many of us go through life taking for granted most of the things someone else has been praying for. We never celebrate our victories and/or take time to reflect on all of the things we have to be grateful for on a daily basis. If you are not currently where you want to be or where you expected to be in life, take a moment and think about all of the wonderful things you currently have to be grateful for. How did that make you feel? As you focus your energy on things, you will attract more things, experiences, and memories to be grateful for.

I once read that you should live your life as a thank you. Being grateful will lead to positive thoughts and feelings, which will increase your quality of life. You will need to be intentional about your use of gratitude in your daily life. You can have a more fulfilling life by using the power of gratitude. If you are looking for a personal, spiritual, mental, and/or physical transformation, I urge you to use the power of gratitude.

Compiled by Kate Gardner

This is not the end

This is just the beginning ☺

About The Missing Piece

The Missing Piece Publishing is the creator and publisher of the #1 international best-selling book series; "The Missing Piece" which provides a platform to help authors and online business grow a successful international platform and help them succeed in turning their followers into raving fans that constantly buy from them.

What first started out has an empowerment Facebook page quickly grew into an international publishing company, which created and published a best-selling book series and went on to publish solo author books which also helped create the same success.

In just 2 years The Missing Piece Publishing created over 100 international best-selling authors; it's touched thousands of people's lives all across the world by airing a daily podcast that has already been listened to over 58,000 times, became a sponsor to the upcoming documentary film "Coaching Movie", which is starring the world renowned coaches like Jack Canfield and Marci Shimoff.

www.themissingpiecepublishing.com

www.the-missing-piece.net

Lightning Source UK Ltd.
Milton Keynes UK
UKOW06f1935050116

265873UK00014B/308/P